SAFE,
not *Sorry*

SAFE, not *Sorry*

Keeping Yourself

and Your Family

Safe in a Violent Age

Tanya K. Metaksa

Executive Director
NRA Institute for Legislative Action

ReganBooks
An Imprint of HarperCollinsPublishers

HarperCollins books may be purchased for educational, business, or sales promotional use. For information please write: Special Markets Department, HarperCollins Publishers, Inc., 10 East 53rd Street, New York, NY 10022.

FIRST EDITION

Designed by Ruth Lee

ISBN 0-06-039191-X

97 98 99 00 01 ❖/RRD 10 9 8 7 6 5 4 3 2 1

For Tatiana, Alexandra, and Victoria,
may you always be safe

CONTENTS

CONTENTS

ACKNOWLEDGMENTS

Safe, Not Sorry is based on a collaborative effort to produce a program, Refuse To Be A Victim, that would help today's woman to take responsibility for her own personal safety. The design and implementation of that program would never have happened without the vision and support of the Executive Director of the National Rifle Association, Wayne R. LaPierre, Jr., the women of the NRA Board of Directors, and especially the members of the Women's Policies Committee in 1992–93.

In the writing of this book I have had valuable assistance and insight from many people. I want to thank former and present members of the NRA staff, including Jennifer Cava, Mary Sue Faulkner, John Frazer, Chandra Gribbon, Douglas Gross, Mary Rose Jennison, Jane Johnson, Sonny Jones, James Manown, Mark Overstreet, Bill Parkerson, Elizabeth Swazey, Easter Thompson, and Thomas Wyld for their invaluable suggestions and editorial assistance. Dr. Fran Haga, UNC/Pembroke, provided hours of insight and information and until this very moment didn't know she was assisting a literary project. I am grateful to my literary agent, Keith Korman, for his vision in conceiving such a book. The deft hand of Kristin Kiser, associate editor of Regan Books, helped mold the chapters into a well-organized form. And I am deeply indebted to Jim Bohan for his extraordinary talent.

And last, thanks to my best friend, colleague, and husband, George Metaksa. He has been a bedrock of support in all my life's endeavors, and his steadfast encouragement and support made *Safe, Not Sorry* a reality.

Springfield, Virginia
January 1997

INTRODUCTION

OUR MOST PRIZED POSSESSIONS

It was a beautiful summer day in 1989 at the beach in Connecticut. The humidity was low, the sky clear, only a few fluffy white clouds and the waves splashing gently on the sand. My three daughters, my only granddaughter, and I had decided to have a "girls day out" and spend a lazy day together. I dove through the water and swam out a few hundred feet, then turned and just relaxed, floated. While I floated, I looked back at the most peaceful and precious scene on earth, an image that has become one of the most enduring pictures in my mind.

My daughters, ages twenty-eight, twenty-seven and twenty-five, and my granddaughter, age two, were building sand castles, working in harmony and laughing. It made me proud, and I couldn't help thinking that if today were the last day of my life, I would die happy and content, for upon that beach was the fruit of my life's work.

Life has blessed me with the privilege of raising three wonderful women. Each one is unique and each one a trusted friend as well as a daughter. Not easy. Ever a challenge. The obstacles life puts in our way—illnesses, accidents, financial misfortunes—make raising a family difficult at best.

As I floated through the gentle waves, I thought about my own childhood and the overwhelming challenges my parents had to face. At the time I didn't understand and couldn't appreciate the world they confronted. As an adult I understand the enormity of what my family went through to build a better life for me.

My father left his homeland with nothing more than the clothes on his back. He fled Russia eighty-five years ago, poor and on foot, hunted down by the Bolsheviks who would have killed him on sight. He escaped to Paris, then Great Britain, and finally the United States of America to find freedom and a sense of belonging. I was born midway in his journey, in the United Kingdom, the daughter of a theater director and an American dancer.

My mother was a dancer. She ran her own studio in New York from the time she was seventeen, juggling her own dance lessons, rehearsals, and performances with the necessity of earning a living. She met my father and then went to Europe to dance, get married, and have a child.

For two years our life was idyllic. Then the storm clouds of war rolled across Europe. My father barely survived the last European war and had no desire to be caught up in another one. In 1939 we set sail from Paris to New York City. I was two, and sailing evidently didn't set well with me. I became quite ill. My father was frantic, worrying that my illness would keep us from getting into the United States.

Fortunately it did not. However, for the better part of the next year my illness drained their finances. My parents, loving creatures that they were, thought only for my safety and well-being. And as a small child I felt no fear because I was protected by these caring parents.

My two-year-old granddaughter, Nina, playing on the sand under the watchful and loving eyes of her mother and two aunts, felt no fear that summer's day. She had no knowledge of the many looming dangers she could face in her life. Although the tuberculosis that jeopardized my life at her age no longer carries the same threat today, many other illnesses endanger her, not only at this age but potentially throughout her years. Twentieth-century society and science have risen to combat each newly discovered internal threat to our health and well-being. New technology has been utilized in diagnoses, prevention, and eradication. Drugs and surgical techniques have been created, and diets and lifestyle changes have evolved. We need only heed the warnings and avail ourselves of the cures.

Most women are well aware of the threat to their bodies from disease. Approximately a hundred and eighty thousand cases of breast cancer are diagnosed each year through early detection procedures such as self-examination and mammograms. A large percentage of women diagnosed are treated, and go on to live normal or relatively normal lives because they took proper precautions with their health. This, as opposed to the surely one hundred percent who would have died of the disease a scant generation ago.

Cervical cancer is almost always curable if found in its early stages. Women know and understand this, and many have annual Pap smears as a safeguard. Unlike breast cancer, cervical cancer does not strike that many women. Only about fifteen thousand cases are diagnosed in an average year. Yet, because some women are ignorant of or refuse to use the tools at hand to protect themselves, almost five thousand die in the United States each year from a curable disease. It's a tragedy and a waste.

While certainly no one can say that the predator parasites within us are under control, through developed technology and the good sense to use it, the effects of disease destroy a significantly smaller percentage of women than in years past. Keeping an eye to our health is a daily habit, and most of us would no more engage in behavior that puts us at risk than we would walk into a raging blizzard wearing only our underwear.

I have seen medical technology advance. I have participated in education campaigns to inform the public on methods of detection and treatment to eradicate disease. So I feel relatively comfortable that my daughters and granddaughter will use the knowledge that is readily available to protect themselves from as many medical threats as possible.

But as I floated in the water on that summer's day I worried about a different threat. Would the same prevention and eradication techniques be used to keep those playing serenely on the beach free from what has become the greatest threat of our times: the human predator? I wondered what I could do to keep my granddaughter safe in a world where more and more of these predators roam the streets and prey on innocent victims—especially women.

As there are approximately a hundred and eighty thousand diagnosed cases of breast cancer in the United States each year, there are also approximately a hundred and eighty thousand reported incidents of rape in this country. Experts believe an equal number go unreported. Yet the vast majority of women do little to protect themselves from the threat.

Most males don't understand the effects of rape on a woman. There are 60 minutes in an hour, 1,440 in a day, 525,600 in a year, and more than 42,000,000 in a life span of eighty years. The average rape lasts less than 30 minutes. It is difficult for them to understand how a 30-minute event, however traumatic, can impact the remaining 42,000,000. But it does, because rape is not a half hour's occurrence: rape lasts forever. It is more invasive than a bullet wound, and men should remember that a single trigger pull taking much less than a second cannot only stop a beating heart but can change the victim's entire lifestyle and personality.

If the same number of women who have learned how to protect themselves against breast cancer also learned to protect themselves against rapists, how many attempts would be foiled? How many rapes would never even be attempted because the woman recognized the potential danger and avoided it, just as her prehistoric grandmother avoided being eaten by a wild beast?

Approximately five thousand women are murdered each year, a number roughly equal to those who die of cervical cancer. It would be interesting to know how many female murder victims had their yearly Pap smear. Then one could ponder why they chose to protect themselves from one deadly predator parasite but neglected to protect themselves from another.

So as I watched an idyllic scene on the beach that day, I began to think of how I could ensure the safety and protection of not only my three daughters and one granddaughter, but of all women.

That haunting question bothered me for several years. I read about the problems of random violent crime. And the more I read, the more I asked, how does one prepare one's children—especially daughters—for a nightmare that has much too real a chance of becoming reality? According to the Department of Justice, three out of four women are victimized by violent crime in their lifetime.

In 1991 I was elected to the Board of Directors of the National Rifle Association. One year later I became Chairwoman of the NRA Women's Policies Committee. One of the first things on my agenda was to address the issue of violent crime against women to my female colleagues on the Board, and female employees of the NRA and the hundreds of thousands of female members of the NRA.

It soon became apparent that education was one of the answers. We believed that if we taught women prevention techniques, the number of victims of random violent crime would decrease. I discussed the approach with my daughters, who discussed it with their friends and anyone else who would give an opinion. The feedback was unanimous. Women were thirsting for this information, and if such a course were offered, would take the time to attend.

Out of this came the NRA's Refuse To Be A Victim. That program and *Safe, Not Sorry* were conceived to teach today's woman how to take responsibility for her own self-defense. It has always been acceptable for men to defend themselves, to kill those who would steal their property or take their lives or the lives of their families. Wyatt Earp, Jim Bowie, and the like are depicted as masculine role models and icons. There are no similar images for women. Traditionally we've been the natural prey of society's criminal element, so much so that certain classifications of crime apply almost exclusively to women: purse-snatching, spousal abuse, rape, and lust murder.

Today's woman doesn't have to play that deadly game. In World War II the men went to war and the women made the guns that won the victory. When the men marched home, many found their "little girls" had discovered they could survive without them. Red-blooded American men have yet to get over the shock.

Golda Meir, Margaret Thatcher, and Indira Gandhi led great nations in time of peace and time of war. Male aggressors looked at Israel, Britain, and India and thought them easy prey. They were wrong. The women furnished strong leadership and the troops brought home the victory.

Women routinely prove their independence in almost every aspect of life except self-defense. Perhaps it's genetic, perhaps it's social conditioning—who knows? But women have generally been content to abdicate responsibility for their physical safety to government in the form of a police department, or to another individual in the form of whatever male is close at hand. Current society, which is experiencing more and more women living at least part of their lives without men, no longer affords such luxury.

Politicians can demand that people be personally accountable for themselves, but if women do not have the knowledge and the tools to protect themselves, such entreaties are no more than empty rhetoric. Violence may or may not be innate to the human condition, but acting responsibly is learned behavior. We're here to banish the former and encourage the latter. It is in that spirit that the women of the NRA developed this program.

Prepare yourself for some straight talk, for a trip into the world of practical reality. *Safe, Not Sorry* seeks to encourage an attitude in the modern woman that will give her the strength and ability to provide for her own security. That goal will not be accomplished by mincing words. If women spent as much time actually thinking about taking real precautions as they do in preparing their hair and makeup, they would find that they were ready to defend themselves against almost any act of violence. And by being prepared, they might even prevent a violent act.

Our purpose is to give women a practical and rational means of protecting themselves. This book will illustrate situations in which a woman should be aware of the potential for danger and suggest how to deal with it. It will also tell the stories of women who found themselves in mortal danger and had to deal with it and the aftermath, alone. Women who before, during, or after the fact found the strength to take their destiny in their own hands. Women who chose to be safe, not sorry.

ONE

AREAS OF VULNERABILITY

The historian Plutarch attributes the words "know thyself" to the Delphic Oracle. This means that in ancient times the phrase had been around longer than anyone could remember, and probably predated the dawn of written history. One can easily imagine the tribal sage of a prehistoric society sitting around a campfire and explaining all the dangers of their era to the young. When asked how one lives in such perilous times, the elder answers, "First one must know thyself."

In regard to securing your personal safety, nothing has changed. First, you must take a long and objective look at yourself and see exactly what is your current position in life. I say "current" because life is a river, not a block of concrete. As your life flows from one stage to the next, the changes must be recognized and given consideration. Knowing yourself does not require you to form a detailed philosophical approach to the universe or list your goals and aspirations for the first quarter of the next century.

It means to look at your life from an almost journalistic point of view. To understand the *who*'s, *what*'s, *where*'s, *when*'s, *why*'s, and *how*'s of your life.

The "who" of your life isn't just who you are, it's also who are those around you. Women should think about who they're going with or are married to. Are they jealous, do they drink too much, do they have the potential to "lose it" because of anger, stress, or alcohol and could they beat, rape, or kill you because of it? Never forget that the greatest number of crimes against women take place in the home at the hands of someone who claims to love them. You must take a good hard look at those around you, and find the thin and moving line between paranoia and preparedness and cling to it.

The list of "who's" to be considered consists of practically every person you're exposed to on a regular basis. Your boss, if you have one. Fellow workers, the guy who fixes your car, the people you see when you take your morning run, the person who reads the meters at your home. Be aware of them, don't simply assume they're dress extras in the long movie of your life. Notice and evaluate them, because in this movie an extra can preemptively decide to upgrade his part to that of a star and you can suddenly find yourself playing the role of victim to his Freddy Krueger.

Identifying "who" is the most important part of your quest. We will discuss the other elements of the equation in detail as we go deeper into this work, but always remember to keep your eyes on the "who." No one was ever robbed, raped, murdered, or mutilated by a "what," "where," or "when."

"What" is what you do on a day-to-day basis; in essence, the things you do that make you what you are. No one is ever just one thing at any stage of his or her life, so this requires more than casual consideration. You are your job, whatever that is—and it doesn't matter what it is—it's a part of your identity and therefore a part of your vulnerability. While a corporate executive lives in a different world than a social worker and the social worker lives in a different world than a topless dancer, all three have in common the fact they're vulnerable both at work and going to and from it. Obviously the potential for threat varies, but the variations do not afford you the luxury of disregarding them. Your recreation, even if your idea of recreation is eating a bag of popcorn on the couch and watching television, is another part of your identity, another part of your "what." There are other factors.

Suppose some of your "what's" are these: single person who tends bar, enjoys music, likes art, works out, and has no significant other. The "what's" dictate the "when's" and "where's." You are a bartender, so you spend five evenings a week in a bar, working from 7:00 P.M. until 2:00 A.M. It takes you half an hour to close your books, so by 2:30 you're on your way home. It takes another half hour to drive home, so most of the time you're returning home during the darkest hours of night. This part of your "what" has dictated a pattern of extreme vulnerability and this pattern will be noticed by all the major "who's" in your life, the good ones and the bad ones.

Maybe you're like the telephone operator, a young grandmother in her forties, whom I met in Spokane,

Washington. When she finished her shift at 3:00 A.M. each morning, she had to cross a street to get to her car. As she crossed the street and walked across the dark parking lot, she had to thread her way through the local drunks and drug addicts that were dropped off by the Spokane Police Department. The building next to her parking lot was the local detox center.

Or perhaps you like music and art, so you go to clubs at night on your days off, museums in the daytime, before work. Perhaps you take an occasional art lesson. More patterns. You work out at a gym three days a week; from 2:30 P.M. until 4:00 P.M. in the afternoon you are doing low-impact aerobics and working the machines. Patterns.

Since you're a human, you have to eat. That means grocery stores, restaurants, perhaps fast-food places. You are single and you date occasionally. More patterns. More areas of vulnerability.

What is your neighborhood like? Is it reasonably safe, or do shootings occur four times a night? It usually follows that the more affluent the neighborhood, the safer the inhabitants. However, just because you can't afford a million-dollar apartment in a building with more security than the White House doesn't mean you forfeit your right to live. It does mean if you want to have a chance at going through life in relative safety you have to use some sense. You absolutely must be aware of what goes on around you.

Be realistic about the safety of your neighborhood. Most of us want to believe that we live in a safe environment. Women who are queried about the relative safety of their neighborhoods usually minimize the dangers. Not until they are asked about *specific* areas of their environment do they look at their surroundings concretely and realistically.

Look at your life as if you were a predator. If you wanted to rob, rape, carjack, serial-murder, or roast yourself over an open fire, *where* would you do it? This is all connected to the "what's," "where's," and "when's" of your existence.

Add "how" to the above as you expand your awareness. If you were going after you, how would you do it? What is your greatest fear? Largest weakness? The essence of strength is not how strong you are in your areas of greatest competence. It's how well you are able to defend yourself at your most vulnerable. Predators don't attack you when you are strong. They attack when they perceive you are vulnerable—easy prey.

This leaves us with the "why" of the situation and no, that does not mean why do criminals act the way they do. That's a later discussion and has no relevance to your personal situation. When you're attacked, you could care less about why the person is doing it. Your question is, why are you being attacked and how do you survive?

So, why *are* you in this position? If you've done your best to make yourself secure and still get attacked, that's one thing. Perfection may exist as a philosophical concept but I've never seen it on this earth; no matter what you do, the possibility exists that you can be harmed the same way people who never smoke get lung cancer. But if you did not do everything possible to make yourself secure, why didn't you? Were you too busy to take the time? Do you have some kind of death wish? Were you so intimidated by your surroundings you could not? Or are you just telling yourself the odds are that it won't happen to you?

Seventy-five percent of the women in America will have a crime committed against them in their lifetimes. Any way you count it, that's three out of every four. The odds are overwhelming that it not only can happen to you but *will* happen to you at some point in your life. Do not lie to yourself and think otherwise.

Out of self-knowledge comes strength. Out of strength comes a change in demeanor, a difference in body language, a heightened awareness of the world around. Criminals are predators and predators do not attack the strongest beast in the herd. They're looking for a meal, not a battle with a titan. If they see strength and purpose in your walk, if they notice you are clued in to what's happening around you and act as if you can take care of yourself, there's a good chance they will pass you by and look for easier prey. The only way you win a confrontation with a predator without acquiring some scars in the process is to not be attacked in the first place.

Out of self-knowledge and strength and this heightened new awareness evolves your best weapon against criminal attack. It's a little thing called "instinct." We all have instincts; some of us listen to them, some do not. Some people's instincts are more finely tuned than others. In some people they seem not to work at all.

We all know that things register in our minds at different levels of consciousness. My belief is that instinct is simply our senses seeing or recording something we aren't consciously aware we sensed. Perhaps a sound, something seen with the peripheral vision, or a smell. At some level our subconscious signals our brain that something is wrong, leading to that uneasiness in the pit of the stomach, the proverbial "gut feeling."

Immediately after we get the signal, the rational mind takes over and starts to quarrel with it. "There's nothing wrong," it says. "You're a big girl. You don't have anything to be afraid of." Grow up. I know any number of people who say every time they failed to listen to their instincts they got in trouble.

Everyone knows the story about the boy who cried wolf once too often. However, there is a different twist that illustrates the point about listening to instincts. The twist is that the wolf was there each and every time the boy hollered, but when it saw the villagers coming it jumped back in the bushes. When finally the villagers stayed home and ignored the warning, the wolf ate the boy and the sheep.

It's the same with instincts. Listen to them. If suddenly your stomach tells you to flee, then you flee. Better you look like an idiot for following your "gut feeling" a thousand times than to ignore it once and get eaten.

I don't know what definition the dictionary gives for the word "wisdom," because I have my own. It's the accumulation of knowledge, experiences, and instinct blended together in a rational manner to provide for the betterment of life. Knowledge and experience provide us with the "who's," "what's," "where's," "when's," and "how's" of our life. Knowing those answers provides our identity, and knowing our identity puts us in greater touch with our instincts. And the final result puts us on the road to our very personal brand of wisdom.

A wise person recognizes the value of life and seeks to

preserve it while improving its quality. Little on earth improves the quality of life more than providing for one's personal security. Wisdom leads to security and security leads to greater wisdom. I don't know what your goals are in this life. Perhaps you've given them a great deal of thought, perhaps not. I do know that if you make wisdom and security two of your goals and work toward accomplishing them, the quality of your life will improve.

THE CRIMINAL

A criminal is a criminal by definition of law, and the use of the word changes as fast as the laws change. For purposes of this work I'm defining the word "criminal" as a noun meaning a person who commits a crime against one's person or property. When I use the words "criminal act" I mean a violent and/or illegal act against a victim's person or property. Since this effort is directed at promoting awareness among women, I will be generally speaking of crimes against women, and those who commit them.

In the same sense that an old adage cautions against judging books by their covers, do not assume you can recognize a criminal by his or her exterior trappings. One might think it would be a good thing to pass a law requiring all criminals to wear tattoos, single earrings, and ski masks, and to ride a motorcycle. However, since at the core of a criminal's being is a wanton disregard for law, all that would do is assure they all wear Brooks Brothers suits. In this day and time, the guy on the Harley with the tattoo and earring is more likely to be an accounting clerk on his way to a fern bar.

Criminals come in all shapes and sizes and answer to all sorts of names, including "dear" and "daddy." The deadliest of them are those who present a facade of conformity so when they come for you they look just like everyone else. There are many things criminals have in common; outward appearance is not one of those things.

Criminals believe niceness in others equals weakness. The classic example is when you're driving down the road and you see a young girl standing beside her broken-down car. You stop and offer to help; you're being nice. Your "niceness" equals "prey" in the mind of the human predator, who in this case is a young man hiding behind the car, who catches you completely unaware when he jumps out and hits you over the head with a tire iron. Your money, your car, perhaps your life, are lost because while you were trying to be nice you were really being a chump.

That doesn't mean you should not render aid to a stricken motorist, but if you do, be aware that looks may be deceiving. If we allow criminals to dictate our behavior, before long we develop a mind-set that mimics theirs. When that happens, they have won. However, before we take certain actions, we must assay the risks and understand exactly what can happen in such a circumstance.

You've seen these words before and you will see them again as you read this book. Find the thin and moving line between paranoia and preparedness and cling to it.

Another thing to remember is that when you are stuck

by the side of the road because your car has broken down, or have broken your leg riding your bicycle and are looking for help, the person stopping might not be the Good Samaritan. Depending on the level of your difficulty, there may be little you can do about it, but the point should be kept in mind.

A friend of mine who reads crime novels has suggested that a passage from an Elmore Leonard novel makes the point perfectly. In the novel a beautiful young woman is staggering through the park. She's bleeding, her clothes are torn, she's obviously been raped. She falls into the arms of a passing stranger, tells him her story, and begs him for help.

He looks at her and simply says, "Sister, today just ain't your day." And then he rapes her himself.

My friend suggests that these are the coldest words ever written in a novel. The trouble is, they aren't necessarily fiction.

A common thread in male predators is that they do not see women as human beings, but as objects. It's interesting to note that this is a characteristic criminals have in common with racists. Most racists seem to have one or two friends of a minority group they like, people with whom they communicate, perhaps share meals and pass pleasant times. Yet they virulently hate literally every other member of their friend's race, totally without knowing them.

It's the same with the male predator. They often have wives or girlfriends who know nothing about their other activities, or perhaps even aide and abet them. So the fact that Mr. Nice Guy is nice to your girlfriend means absolutely nothing in terms of how Mr. Nice Guy may treat you.

Those who commit crimes against property see you as something placed on earth for their personal enrichment and amusement. The rapist or murderer believes your private parts exist for his pleasure, or as objects against which to act out his insane hatred of women. You may have lived a wonderful life, gone to college, had a career, raised children, and done all the right things. This means nothing to him. He doesn't feel pain when you are hurt, bleed when you are cut, or grieve when you die. You are disposable. You are bathroom tissue, to be used and replaced when you've reached the limit of your utility. Don't ever forget it, don't ever expect mercy or understanding from the criminal element.

Many criminals are constantly seeking opportunities and prey. The fact that the guy who watches you jogging in the park takes no action the first ten times he sees you means exactly nothing. Just because the meter man or pizza delivery boy smiles at you the first few times he comes by doesn't mean he isn't making a mental note of you for future reference. Until someone has passed whatever criteria you set for your own personal comfort and security, stay alert. After they've passed your tests, still stay alert. It's good practice.

Criminals are walking contradictions, in that while they generally possess low self-esteem they are overconfident about beating you or the system. The overconfidence comes, perhaps, from the fact that you, as a citizen, have a code of ethics by which you abide. The criminal has none. He is totally unencumbered by the societal rules and restraints that govern the activities of most of us. As such, he has no stopping place.

For example, when kids on a school ground get in a fight, they flail away and nothing much happens, but then suddenly one has a bloody nose. This usually stops the fight because they're really just blowing off steam and frustration, not trying to hurt each other. That's not the case in a confrontation with a criminal, as he has little to lose from escalating the situation.

He knows if he gets caught, chances are not much will happen. Most likely the case will never come up in court. If it does, he can inform on someone else and get off with a slap on the wrist if not scot-free, or plea-bargain his case down to a lesser charge. That's if he can't make bail, jump it, and just disappear. Most criminals consider incarceration the same way an investor thinks of lost capital: simply one of the risks of the business.

While they are supremely confident in beating the system and victimizing you, they are underconfident in almost all other areas of their lives. This is why they spend so much time either plying their trade or lining up their next victims. It's the only time they feel like the superior creature they tell themselves they are.

It's also why so many of them demean their victims. It's not enough just to rob or rape or kill, the victim has to be abused, mutilated, and reduced to minus zero. The greater the dehumanization of the victim, the more the criminal feels he gains in self-worth. The greater your pain, the greater his sense of exhilaration. Which means that, putting it in basic terms, the prime mover for many classes of criminal activity is not the criminal's gain but your pain. The reward is in the act itself, the adrenaline rush, the psychological gratification, not the money in your purse. Why else would a burglar feel the need to defecate on the floor or his victim's bed? The criminal loves his work.

While we're speaking in generalities, one must not forget that each criminal is an individual, the same as anyone else.

Some are better or worse than others, some will do this but won't do that, some are totally without restraint. In any confrontation you must be able to intuitively read the individual attacker and respond accordingly. There are cases in which the victim told the attacker about having children or a family and the guy let them go. On the other hand, there are instances where similar stories got people hurt because the criminal's attitude was, "I didn't have a family, why should you?" In such a situation, especially if it's over an extended period of time, you have to be capable of anticipating the unpredictable. This brings us back to instinct.

A number of factors can contribute to making criminals the way they are. They could have come from backgrounds of abuse or poverty or both; they could have had little education. Recent studies indicate a large part of the problem may reside in the gene code or in brain chemistry.

I have as much empathy for abuse victims as anyone. I loathe the abuser, and someday someone might convince me to advocate the death penalty for those who sexually abuse children. BUT, the fact that people have been abused does not give them license to act out their aggressions on those in society who have done them no harm. Nor does it allow them to abdicate responsibility for their actions to the world at large.

Once victims cross the line and become predators, any and all sympathy and understanding due them in their victim status is forfeit. Period. What the above boils down to is a very simple fact. I don't give a damn why they do what they do, I am only looking for ways to keep them from doing it. And this is why:

Criminals, predators, people on the wrong side of ethical behavior have values that are completely antithetical to the rest of us. Show them a picture of a family and ask them to pronounce it good or bad. Chances are, they'll have a negative reaction because, given their personal history, family means pain. Show them a picture of a kicked-in door with an old woman lying beaten on the floor, her purse ripped to shreds, and the reaction will likely be positive. The scene means someone just like them got in, got the money, and got away.

You and I have the opposite reaction. Those among us who didn't know the joy of a family growing up can, at the very least, appreciate the value of one, if not hope to one day have one. None of us would have a positive response to the pain, suffering, or death of an innocent victim.

But to most criminals, there is no such thing as an innocent victim. In their world there are only two classifications of people, predators and prey. If you are female and don't know which of these categories you fall into, there is a seventy-five percent chance that at some time in your life a predator will teach you.

You must also be aware of the environment in which a criminal attack may take place. Obviously, you cannot choose the time of a conflict. That's solely up to the bad guy. Just as obviously, many attacks occur in physical situations outside of your control, on the street, in an elevator. However, many of these attacks take place in locations that should be under your control, such as your car or your home. *Safe, Not Sorry* will strive to teach you how to protect those places, how to tilt any possible confrontation in your favor.

THREE

HOME SECURITY

Think of an onion and relate it to your home security. An onion exists in layers. You have to peel away one to get to the next. That's the way we suggest structuring home security. We want the criminal to have to peel his way through so many layers of security that somewhere in the process he says to heck with it, this is too tough, and goes next door. A whole variety of home security devices are available, from very simple to extremely complex, but the main thing is to layer your house with different things, creating enough obstacles to send the wolf back into the forest.

LOCKS

The first layer of security is your locks. All locks should be dead bolts made of case-hardened steel with bolts that extend at least an inch and a half into the wall. The strike plate—that's the metal piece set into the wall, which the bolt passes through—should be set with screws three inches long, enabling the bolt to pass through the door jamb and into the wall studding. All locks should be double-keyed double-cylinders, so you enter and exit by turning a key.

Yes, this is inconvenient, made even more so by the fact you should never leave the key in the door if you have those pretty and easy-to-break panes of decorator glass in your door or the wall next to it. It also poses a potential problem in case of fire. For this reason, you must keep a key secured but easily accessible to you and your loved ones near each door.

The reason for double-keyed, double-cylinder locks is obvious. If your interior lock has a "throw," the mechanism you simply turn to lock the door from the inside, all some-one has to do is break the entryway glass, or in the case of some frame houses and apartments, poke a hole through the wall, reach in, and unlock the door. It's quicker and easier than you might think.

When you move to a new house or apartment the first thing you need to do after unloading the vans is rekey the locks. Change them if they aren't up to the quality described above. If you are a renter and your landlord doesn't like it, tell him to learn to love it. You can replace your lock with their old one when you move.

It makes no sense to put a top-flight lock in a ten-cent door. Doors should be either metal or solid wood with a metal frame. They should seat well into the frame, fit tightly enough so someone can't get a hacksaw blade between the door and frame and saw through the lock's bolt or the door's hinges. This is true for all exterior doors, not just the front door. Don't forget the door to the garage. Just because you have a heavy automatic garage door doesn't mean you can ignore that inside entryway into your home.

Change the setting on your automatic garage door opener when you move to a new house. People buy the doors, install them, and leave the factory settings in place. This practice is not only ridiculous but life-threatening. All settings are the same when they leave the factory. All the bad guy has to do is drive down the street with his remote control set to factory specs, and sooner or later a door will open.

If you have glass inserts, cover them with metal grill-work. Laws now require such fixtures to be fire-safe, so you no longer have to worry about burning to death in the event of a fire that blocks passages to doors.

Sliding glass doors give you wonderful access to your backyard and patio, but they are a freeway entrance ramp to a burglar. Metal bars keep the door from being forced open along the track but do not keep it from being lifted off the track. There are many different varieties of locks that hold the doors in place and most are very effective. However, there is nothing to stop a burglar from picking up a flower pot, smashing the door, and walking right in. If you gather from the tone used in discussing them that I don't like sliding glass doors, you are correct.

Something else causes me to get upset when I think of it: pet doors. People will put all sorts of sophisticated security in and around their home, then throw it all away by putting a hole in an entrance large enough for a Saint

Bernard to waddle through. If the dog were trained for security it might make some sense, but it's usually the type of mutt who could only hurt an intruder if it licked him to death. Please, please pay attention to this. No one wants to rob your children of their right to romp with Rover or bound with Bowser, but make them responsible for the animal. Unless your dog can use an entranceway small enough to deny access to a housebreaker, do not put a pet door anywhere in your home.

We also suggest building a "safe room" in your home. This is a room with the same kind of locks as your exterior doors, in which you can secure yourself in case of intrusion. What room you choose should be determined by your own needs. If you have no children, the master bedroom is the logical choice, but if you have kids you might want to choose one of their rooms. If you are attacked, gather the family and secure yourselves in that room and call for help. If at all possible, keep a cellular phone in the room. Be sure to periodically check the cell phone battery to make sure it is charged.

Mentioning the cellular phone brings me to a point that will be made several times in these pages. A lot of what is suggested is costly. Some, of course, is not, but much of it requires spending cash. Obviously, if you can't afford some of what is suggested, that's that. However, if it's a matter of spending for security and spending for something you can do without, get the security. You may not need it except for only one day in your life, but when that day comes, if it so much as saves a moment of pain on the part of someone you love or yourself, you will thank God you spent the money.

LIGHTING

The next layer of the onion is lighting. Remember that darkness aids and abets criminal activity, so to be safe you have to take the darkness away from him. When you're not home we suggest using lighting to create an illusion. For not much money you can buy a series of timers that will simulate activity in your home. Lights come on at various times for different periods, the stereo or television can be turned on or off, and so on.

This is not something you do in just one portion of your house at the same time every day. That's a trap people fall into. Stagger the lighting. It's rare for any of us to come home at exactly the same minute every day and turn on the exact same lights in perfect sequence. If, by chance, a criminal is watching your house and the same light turns on in the same room at the same time every day and then turns off an hour later, you might as well hang a neon sign on your front door that says, "Rob me, there's no one home!"

Set timers in the rooms you use, living room, kitchen, den, and bedroom. If your bathroom has an outside window, set a timer to turn on the lights for ten minutes during the middle of the night as if you were regularly getting up for a drink of water or to use the bathroom. Be creative. Look for patterns in what you're doing, avoid them, and give the criminal a little extra to think about.

In an ideal world we would all have 360-degree lighting around our house so that there would be no place for an intruder to hide and not be bathed in light. After my mother's house had been broken into by teenagers, my daughter and I got together and had periphery lighting installed around the house. The lights automatically come on when there is motion around the house or when a car comes down her long driveway. The lights are so sensitive that the family cat walking outside will turn them on. In addition a small beep alerts my mother to any car coming down her driveway at any time of the day. This lighting and alarm system is expensive, both in the cost of installation and monthly electric bills, but it has given my mother, who lives alone, peace of mind, which is priceless. Not everyone can afford such a system, but most people can afford to put single motion detectors on their property.

A motion detector light costs between $20 and $30. Install them covering the entrances to your property and the house itself. Set them to cover your doors, pathways, and low windows. Also use them to illuminate potential hiding places on the property, such as blind corners and large shrubs. This serves two purposes. One, if an intruder comes slinking around the house, as soon as he steps into the area covered by the motion detector he is covered in light. Not only does this greatly displease him, if you see an outside light go on you know something may be threatening your home and can act accordingly.

The second reason for motion detectors is to light your way when you come home after dark. You don't have to worry about turning on lights. If you see other parts of the property illuminated, you are alerted to potential problems, and your general stress level diminishes because you've taken steps toward rendering a potentially dangerous situation neutral. And it is easier to get your house key into the lock on the door.

They also come in handy when your teenage daughter comes home late at night with that guy you're not too sure of. They drive up, the lights come on. She complains, you shrug your shoulders and say it's part of the security system, you don't know how to change it.

If you have areas you want illuminated all night long, there are inexpensive photoelectric cells that you can screw directly into light sockets, then screw the lightbulb into the cell. You can adjust the light sensitivity levels to determine when the lights should automatically illuminate. They're called "dusk to dawn" lights and they're very effective, especially for people who work late.

At the risk of being redundant, it is extremely important to keep your property well lighted, if not all night long then in the manner described. The journey from your car to your house in the dark of night can be one of the longest walks on the planet.

If you have shrubs, keep them well trimmed so they are not capable of concealing a man-sized figure. If you must have large shrubs, cover them with motion detectors. There are also situations where shrubs can work for your benefit. If you have a nice big bay window through which someone can clock the goings-on in your house, plant rose bushes or pyrocanthia in front of it. Not only does it make it difficult to see through, but if an intruder decides to break that window and enter your house he'll garner some scratches on the way in.

But you must keep your bushes trimmed and lit. That beautiful ten-foot-tall piece of greenery by your front door is just perfect for someone to hide behind and grab you as you're on your way into your house.

Make sure when you're not at home your drapes or blinds are closed. While it's nice to have an open, airy house, it is an invitation to criminals to take inventory of everything in your house that they might want to come back and take for themselves.

HOME ALARMS

Alarm systems run the gamut from little battery-operated door alarms to full perimeter systems that are monitored by a third party, 24 hours a day, 365 days a year, with uniformed guards in patrol cars.

The least expensive alarm system is to have none at all but to put up a sign saying "This property is protected by X Security Company." I have no idea how many people do that or how effective it is, but either a lot of people are doing exactly that or many security companies are making serious money. If there is a security patrol that drives through your area it might be effective. Unless someone has checked out your house pretty carefully, they would have no idea whose house the patrol is clocking.

You can also buy a decoy video monitor for about $30. It uses a flashlight battery and has a small blinking red light like a regular security camera. You install it so it appears to be covering your doors or windows. Supposedly the criminal will see the light, assume he's on "Candid Camera," and head for the hills. You can also buy fake sensors for your windows that look like regular alarm sensors but are really decoys. While these appear very realistic, my reaction to things like this is, let the buyer beware. These products don't do anything, they only look like they do something. My concern is that they engender a feeling of security on the part of the homeowner that's not justified by reality.

There are inexpensive battery-operated alarms you can hang on your doors or windows. When the door or window is opened they set off an alarm. There are also motion detectors you place inside the doors or windows that do the same thing once someone enters their area.

The more complicated systems are monitored, meaning they are watched by people trained to evaluate the threat to your property. The biggest thing you want to look for in such a system is that the lights go on and alarm goes off. Law enforcement tells us that silent alarms are good but only for businesses. In your home, you want to use whatever is at your disposal to get the bad guy out of your world as soon as possible. Loud noise and lights are a good way to get that process started.

In evaluating monitored systems we once again look to our old friends, the words "when," "who," and "how." You want to know when the company is monitoring your place. If there is a security patrol, when does it patrol? "Who," again, is extremely important. Have the personnel been checked out and are they competent? Where are they located? Are they sitting in New Mexico with a large switchboard or do they have an office in your area? Do they send a car or do they call the police? Do they call you to see if there is a problem and you give them a code word if everything is okay? Be sure you understand who has the ultimate responsibility for checking your house.

Many of these services are hooked into your telephone

lines and can be circumvented by cutting phone service. To account for this, many security companies are burying telephone lines when they install the service and others are going to radio-wave communication. The best thing to do is check out the alarm company with other users and the local Better Business Bureau, then determine the particulars of the service with the service provider.

Before the company comes out to tell you about their service you need to figure out exactly what it is you want protected. Define your perimeter. Is it the house, from the driveway, the property line?

Some of the equipment available today is highly sophisticated. Don't let that word frighten you; it doesn't necessarily mean it's difficult to use. Interior alarms react to motion, heat, and sound. When the alarm is on and someone moves or makes a sound, the alarm is activated. The heat sensors are particularly useful because they cover two areas, fire and theft. If something 98.6 degrees Fahrenheit walks by the heat sensor it sets off the alarm, but the alarm also works if an electrical line starts to smolder or some form of spontaneous combustion occurs. So you're protected in case of fire as well as theft.

You can also buy this kind of protection for the entire house or for certain areas. For example, if you only want it to protect your crown jewels, equipment can be calibrated to cover that specific area.

A lot of companies now have what is called a "panic button," which is usually kept by the bed for use in case of a nighttime emergency. Most of the time when a security company receives a call, it will call back the client to verify an emergency before contacting help. When they receive a panic button signal, this procedure is bypassed and help is immediately called or sent.

If your system has a control panel device that is battery operated, make sure you have a backup battery for it. Also, if your control panel is near the door, make sure your siren is located elsewhere. Otherwise, when an intruder comes through the door all he has to do is grab it and rip out the wires and your alarm system is toast.

There are magnetic sensors for doors and windows. These consist of two magnets that form a single circuit when they're in contact with each other. When the circuit is broken, an alarm is activated. The problem with these devices is that in the case of windows, someone can simply break out the pane without interrupting the magnetic circuit. To solve this problem, magnetic circuits should be used in tandem with pressure-sensitive devices. When any form of pressure is exerted against the pane, the vibration activates an alarm. These are small, quarter-sized metal pieces and are applied directly to the glass.

None of this does any good if you happen to have your windows open, but a recent development covers this. Security wires can be woven into the mesh wire of your screens. If the screens are cut or removed, an alarm is activated. This combination of magnetic contacts, pressure-sensitive devices, and wired screens affords reasonably good security. But according to a report in the major metropolitan are where I live, security systems can have an expensive downside. Ninety-five percent of the time when the police or security company show up, they find no cause for alarm. The system has just gone haywire.

False alarms are now becoming such a dangerous and expensive problem to municipalities that many governments are making it more difficult for a homeowner to own and use security systems. They are making alarm owners, both homeowners and businesses, register their alarm systems, as well as imposing fines. For example, in Montgomery County, an upscale bedroom community near Washington, D.C., there were 40,485 false alarms out of a total of 40,967 alarm calls in one year. As a result, the county now imposes fines for false alarms. After the third false alarm the fine is $50 and then the fines increase rapidly. The fifteenth false alarm is a pricey $1,000. If you own a business, the twentieth false alarm will cost you $4,000. Other counties in the D.C. metropolitan area, with the exception of D.C. itself, are following suit. The problem appears to be alarm owners who do not know how to operate their systems properly, equipment that may be too complicated for the owner, and weather that can play havoc with alarms. So be aware that your alarm may cause you more trouble if you do not take precautions.

Then there is the old standby, the portable, fur-wearing, Alpo-eating security system called a dog. Dogs have senses that are much more acute than humans and can be an effective early warning system. If that's all you are using them for, it doesn't matter the size or breed. Those of you who have or have had dogs know you can be enjoying a quiet moment and suddenly the dog will sense something and react. The trouble is, unless the dog is trained, it could easily be reacting to the neighbor's cat or have caught a scent of something else of great interest to dogs and not at all to humans.

Dogs that are extensively trained require firm handling. It must be understood that a trained dog ceases to be primarily a pet, but is there to provide a service. If you have such a dog don't forget what it is there for, because if you do you lose control of the animal. You should also be aware that if you have a trained dog your home liability carrier may increase your premiums, as insurers consider them an enhanced risk.

The downside of dogs—if you aren't a dog lover—is that they require time, affection, and care. A cat lover friend of mine calls them "manure factories." However, there is a dramatic upside as well. A survey was taken in a state prison where burglars were asked if there was a single factor that would make them abandon one house and try for another. A large percentage of them answered yes. What was the single factor that would drive them away?

A dog.

KEYS

Keep your house keys separate from the rest of your life. When you use valet parking or leave your car with a mechanic, there is no reason in the world to give away the keys to everything else you own. This is especially important when it comes to car mechanics. Your name and address are written on a piece of paper, put on a clipboard, and hung on a nail with your keys. It's an open invitation for someone to grab them, make a copy or a wax impression, jot down your address, and steal you out of house and home at their convenience. All the home security in the world is valueless if you don't use just a little bit of common sense in the other areas of life. Cut yourself a valet key and use it. If you give your coat to a coat check person at a restaurant, don't leave your keys in the coat. Don't leave them in your desk at the office. Put them in your purse or pocket.

If you have to hide a key around the house, don't be obvious. Don't put it on the top of the door frame or under the flower pot. Above all, think. There are any number of devices one can buy for hiding keys around the house. My favorite one is a dog collar that has a space for a key in it. If you have a Doberman, you have a truly safe place to hide your spare house key.

When you buy a product to hide an outside key, however, remember that professional housebreakers make a study of security products. You might be better off to find your own hiding place. Just remember to be creative about it.

Since we have already suggested that you keep the keys to your home separate from your many other keys, make sure that as you walk toward your home, you have your house key ready to use. I have my house key distinguished from my other keys with a rubber key cover on it. In that manner, even if it is dark, I can feel which is my house key without fumbling around. Because of this small trick, I always beat my husband in opening the door when we come home at night together.

VISITORS

Remember that anyone who comes to your door who does not reside within the walls of your home is a visitor, and should be on your property with your permission or not at all. If you're a renter reading this and saying to yourself, "I don't own any property," think again. As long as you pay rent according to the agreement between you and the landlord, that's your domicile and you say who comes and goes. It doesn't matter who they are, parent, old boyfriend, boss, or total stranger. It doesn't matter if it's someone you let sleep over the night before and it doesn't matter if they slept on the couch or somewhere else.

If they don't live with you, they are in your domicile with your permission or not at all. Never forget it.

In order to control who comes and goes, or at least to know who's asking to enter, use a wide-angle door viewer. It's essentially like a peephole, except that a peephole affords a limited view. The wide-angle viewer lives up to its name and allows you to see not only a much wider view but also all the way to the ground. The advantage is obvious.

The best device is a video camera with a monitor by the door so you can see not only who's at the door but who's in the area. They're no longer as expensive as they used to be. You can get a decent unit for less than $200.

Of course, it doesn't matter if you have a Swiss Guard standing outside your door if you don't use a little sense about whom you allow inside. I'm not going to spend a lot of time on domestic matters, but suffice it to say, if you had to have your significant other arrested the night before because he got drunk and beat you senseless, and now he's back at the door saying he wants to explain or apologize, don't let him in. Not only don't let him back in the door, don't let him back in your world.

There are some areas of life in which there are no second chances. There are some people who simply do not deserve to be in your presence. If the other person in your life brings you violence, get rid of him or her the first time it happens. Don't rationalize it, don't try to understand it or explain it to yourself, don't let yourself get conned. Get that person out of your life, forever, and do it immediately. If you give them a second chance, you have entered into a hierarchical struggle for dominance that will only see the situation escalate to the point of potential mortality. The promises of renewed love and vows to "never do it again" are not worth your life. If you think they are, give this book to someone else. It's of no value to you.

When strangers come to your door, verify their identity before allowing them entry. If you want a vacuum cleaner, you can buy one just as good and probably for less money at an appliance store instead of from the salesman ringing your doorbell. If you collect those cute little bottles and the Avon Lady shows up at your door, make sure she's not with a housebreaker who has just been released on parole and is standing just outside your view. If you want to meet the Avon Lady or any other person in your home, make an appointment. When you set the time and date, you are in control and are not just answering the door for an unexpected guest.

If a delivery person shows up, or the gas man, phone man, cable TV guy, or anyone else who thinks he has to enter your home, verify who he is. If he's in a uniform, so what? Uniforms can be bought or stolen. Ask for a picture identification card. If he's legitimate, he won't object. If he is with a company and you can see the street, look to see if there is a properly marked vehicle parked in front of your house. That includes police officers. "Uniforms R Us" sells to anyone with money, and a badge can be bought at a pawn shop. Ask to see a picture ID. If he has an ID, but you're still uneasy, ask where he's from and who is the watch commander. Then call and find out if there is supposed to be an officer at your door. Most police officers will understand. Impostors will disappear.

The biggest credential in the world is a clipboard. Let a guy dressed nicely come by the average home or apartment with a clipboard in his hand, and he consistently gains admittance. People assume the clipboard means this guy is working, taking care of some kind of business. Bad guys know this better than you do, and an astounding number of them use the ploy.

President Ronald Reagan said his motto in dealing with the Soviets was "Trust but verify." With strangers at your door there is no need to extend trust. Your motto should be one word: "Verify!"

Also remember that the person you're talking to is not necessarily the only person who's hearing your words. If you're going to take a trip and leave your house empty, don't hold court at the salon and tell the stylist all about it. He or she may be an old and dear friend, but do you know the person sitting in the next chair? Or the person in the booth behind you at the coffee shop? Or the next person in line at the grocery store? Old-time fishermen have a saying: "Even a fish would stay out of trouble if he kept his mouth shut." Consider applying those words to your personal safety.

Think about getting a mailbox service. This is important in case you lose your purse or whatever you carry your keys and identification in. If it's found by a thief or a rapist, there is nothing to lead him back to your home. It's also good because mail doesn't accumulate. Mail falling out of a mailbox is a neon sign to a housebreaker that says "Rob me!" Remember to get all of your licenses, magazine subscriptions, and other mail changed over to the service. It also eliminates one person on the home delivery list, because that way you know if a mailman comes to your house he's not a mailman.

If you're going out of town for an extended stay, be sure to make arrangements to have your lawn mowed and to cancel your newspaper subscription. Try not to leave a message on your answering machine that says, "Hi, Joe and I and the kids are out of town for a year. We took the Doberman with us so it's perfectly safe for you to come over and make yourself at home."

I realize it's unlikely everyone who reads these pages will follow every suggestion enclosed. Some of you can't afford the cost; others may not feel the problem is as serious as others do. However, let's assume for the moment that someone follows this program to a T. They buy all the gizmos and go through all the self-learning and situation-preparation scenarios. They do everything but one simple thing. They don't use it.

Home security devices are just like that StairMaster machine you've got sitting in the corner of the guest room gathering dust. The knowledge you gain of yourself is just like that French course you took when you thought you were going to spend a summer on the Riviera. They aren't worth a fig if you don't use them.

While many criminals may suffer from low self-esteem and may be overconfident about their ability to take what is yours, don't ever make the mistake of thinking they're dumb. People who commit crimes know they live in a changing world, and they change their operating procedures accordingly.

An example would be carjacking. Ten years ago you never heard about carjackings, then along came better auto security devices, and the Club, and all sorts of things. Next thing you knew, carjackings were rampant because it's easier to steal a car from someone parked at a stoplight listening to talk radio than it is to beat an alarm.

Home invaders are learning the same lesson. Many of them are finding it much easier to break into a house with the family at home and do whatever they care to do than beat today's sophisticated alarm systems. Which means that you can't stop being aware just because you've got your feet propped up and are watching "Dr. Quinn, Medicine Woman" on Saturday night.

It's a crying shame that in this day and age we pay taxes to support police functions on a federal, state, county, and city level and still have to be concerned with our own security. It's even worse that, after installing locks and other devices, we really can't relax in our own abode.

During my childhood in Connecticut, everyone in our neighborhood left their doors unlocked whether they were home or not. In the summertime, windows were open all over the house to catch the cooling breezes. However, in today's America, everyone should lock their doors whether they are home or not, and windows that are accessible from the ground should not be left open for an uninvited guest to climb through.

Unfortunately, that's the nature of today's society. Be aware or you'll be a victim of it.

In the final analysis, clearly understand that YOU are far and away your most effective home security device. Which is appropriate because you and your family are the ones who will pay the price if criminal activity knocks at your door.

F O U R

TRAVEL SECURITY

If you must travel alone, set an itinerary and abide by it if at all possible. Call the hotels you'll be using and ask questions. Ask them about their security. Do they have around the clock personnel seeing to your safety? Ask what kind of keys they use for guest rooms. Are they old-style metal keys or has the hotel upgraded to disposable magnetic cards? Where will your room be? Ground level? The end of a hall? If you arrive and find they've placed you on the ground floor, ask for another room. Also, a lot of hotels have banquet areas on the lower floors with wraparound balconies that are public walkways. If you find yourself in such a room you might as well be on the ground. Ask for another room.

Check out their exterior lighting and the security of their parking lot, especially if you're going to be in and out a lot. Check the locks on the doors; you want them to be as secure as those in your home. Be sure they are dead bolts with a chain and a manual lock on the inside of the door.

Know where the exits are. This is for two purposes; if there is someone in your room and you need to flee, or in case of fire.

Be sure there is a phone in the room. Believe it or not, there are still places that do not have phones in every room.

Make sure their desk is staffed twenty-four hours a day in case you have a late-night emergency. Preferably the place should have twenty-four-hour security as well.

When you check in, watch out that the clerk doesn't announce you. "Okay, Miss Jones, you're in room 724, too bad your boyfriend couldn't come with you." Don't laugh, it happens. If it does, quietly ask the clerk to assign you another room and to be a bit more discreet.

Make sure you aren't given a metal key with your room number stamped into it in case you lose it. It's better to stay in a place with magnetic keys. Law enforcement uniformly agrees they're safer.

Be careful when you rent a car. Many of the rental car agencies no longer put bright neon signs on their cars advertising their ownership by the renting agency. Several years ago in Florida, tourists were robbed and murdered by carjackers who identified them by the rental cars they were driving. Question the agency before you rent. Do they mark their cars? If so, is it blatant or discreet? The smaller the markers are the better—some agencies use ones that are not easily identifiable. If they tell you there is a big bumper sticker with their name on it in flashing lights, go to a different agency.

There are a number of personal safety devices you can

travel with, such as alarms and sprays. These will be discussed in more detail in a later section. If you carry pepper spray or other means of self-protection, remember that the laws vary from state to state. What is legal in Texas may be a misdemeanor or even a felony in California. Be sure you know the laws in the area you're traveling through, otherwise you may find you have to spend substantially more time there than you anticipated.

Don't forget your home when you're on the road. If you have neighbors with an extra car, consider asking them to park it in your driveway when you're gone. If you live in an apartment, turn down the ringer on your phone and your answering machine. A phone that continuously rings and rings without being answered or is always answered by a machine signals that you're away. I'll repeat, don't forget to arrange for the lawn to be mowed, or the sidewalk shoveled if you live where it snows.

If possible, have neighbors deposit trash in your receptacles. I know this sounds funny, but if the trash man comes by once or twice a week and there is no garbage to collect, it tells him you aren't home. There was a recent case of a burglary ring that was linked back to trash collectors. One or more of the garbage collectors in the area were in league with some thieves and chose their targets accordingly.

The trash example simply indicates that for as many areas of vulnerability we can identify and bolster, there is always another one that's been missed. All you can do is the best you can. In most cases it's enough. When it's not, be sure you're insured.

FIVE

PHONE SECURITY

Your telephone provides an excellent source of information and amusement for criminals. Most of us fall into the trap of thinking that since the person speaking is on the other end of a fiber-optic line, they pose no physical danger to our safety. While that may be true at the moment the conversation is taking place, it may not hold true over the long term.

INFORMATION SCAMS

Phones have been used since their inception by con artists to separate the naive from their money. Currently there are cons going on that fall into a gray area between phone and mail. The mail brings a notification telling you you've won a prize. To claim it you must call a 900 number; it costs X dollars a minute to do so. After several minutes that cost you $20 or $30, you find you've won a dollar. A few days later a check for a dollar arrives in the mail. Try not to spend it all in one place.

There are others. Fund-raising for police events is a popular one. Most people want to support their local police. However, some so-called police fund-raisers lead you to believe that if you buy a couple of tickets, you'll get a special bumper sticker and the next time you get stopped you won't be cited. So you send a check, and instead of supporting your local sheriff you're supporting your local phone scammer. If you get a call asking you to buy tickets to this or that to benefit police, call your area police and verify that this is a legitimate activity.

Phone scammers exist in multitudes, and a new scam is invented daily. There is the one about the oil wells, the gold mine, the commodities, the stock options—the list goes on and on. There are tons of people out there who want nothing more than to separate you from your money, and your telephone is their fast track into your wallet. If you want to use your telephone to buy things, that's your business and that's fine. But buy from people whom *you* call. Don't buy from people who call you.

Phone surveys may not separate you from your money during the call but they can have the same results later on. Criminals use this method to find out when you're home, what you earn, who lives there, or what you have that they might want. Obviously they won't say, "This is Housebreaker's Inc., what do you have that I might like to steal?" But they might represent themselves as the local library association and tell you they're looking at the possibility of expanding the book list and they'd like to assay public opinion on the subject. So they find out what you read, who else in the family might use the service, and other information. By the end of the conversation they know enough about you and your habits to know if they want to break into your house or not.

Before you give out any information over the telephone, know to whom you're talking. The best practice is to tell them to send you their questionnaire and a letter on their letterhead requesting the information. If they want your address, tell them to get it out of the phone book.

Speaking of the phone book, it's a good idea to list your phone in another name. If your name is Jones and your phone is listed as Smith, when you get a call asking for Ms. Smith you know it's a call from a stranger. Act accordingly. And you do not have to put an address in the phone book. Ask the phone company to list you only by the town in which you live. The phone company may not want to do that, but they will comply if you ask.

If you have an answering machine or voice mail, leave a generic message. If you live alone, recruit a male friend or acquaintance to record a message for you. The message should say, "We can't come to the phone, please leave a message." There is no need to identify yourself, or answer with your phone number. If the caller doesn't know whom they're calling, that's their problem. Do not put on your sexiest voice and announce to the world you're in Bora Bora distributing medicine to the natives and won't be back until the summer solstice.

If you use a phone card, be careful how and where you use it. There is a thriving cottage industry in stealing calling card numbers, and you can find yourself with an unpleasant surprise on your bill at the end of the month. When you punch in your code, guard it the same way you would guard your PIN on an ATM. Cover the fingers used to punch in the code with your free hand.

HARASSMENT CALLS

There are several unprofitable ways for individuals to amuse themselves on the telephone that can be irritating, and in some cases, outright dangerous. They are prank calls, obscene calls, and harassing calls.

There's little to prank calls other than aggravation. Usually these are from kids playing, and they're easy to ignore. If they continue, you might want to talk to the phone company about it, but they generally are not a problem. If they escalate, that's another matter.

Obscene calls are also an aggravation and for the most part are nothing much to worry about, since nothing usually comes of them. Unless they disturb you past the point of toleration, the best thing to do is simply to hang up as soon as you figure out what they are, and ignore them. Granted, the person is saying things you don't want to hear, but if you don't listen to him it won't be long before he calls someone else. If he escalates the situation, then the calls cross the line and become harassment, and that's another matter.

When someone calls you continually, is obscene, tells you he loves you, threatens you, perhaps describes something he's seen you doing, you know you've encountered more than just the garden variety telephone idiot. It's time to do something. Call the police and let them handle it.

If they feel the situation warrants it, they may set up a trace, monitor, or log your calls. The police usually will tell you to immediately hang up when such a call comes in. As soon as you recognize the call for what it is, hang up. Don't talk, don't reason, don't do something cute like blow a whistle, don't do something that might make the situation worse than it is. Hang up.

You may want to check out some of the newer services from the phone companies. Caller ID works nationally in most areas and is effective. Call Block is a service that blocks a specified number from calling your machine. If you are the recipient of prank or obscene calls, identify the calling number with Caller ID, report it, and use Call Block to shut out future calls from that number. If kids are playing games, you might want to call their parents and tell them.

CELLULAR PHONES

I have one thing to say about cellular phones: get one and take it with you wherever you go. They are excellent security devices. If your car breaks down you can call for help. If you're walking around or jogging and are harassed or otherwise run into trouble, you can call 911. If you're in your house and someone breaks in after cutting standard telephone lines or simply taking your phone off the hook, you still have a viable means of communication at hand.

Remember, however, that when you call 911 you need to be sure where the call is going. If you are traveling and call 911 your phone may be programmed to phone 911 in your local area, not 911 in the area you're physically in.

Cellular phones are great for reporting crimes in progress and updating authorities as to what's going on. In Florida one of the phone companies donated a number of units to a Neighborhood Watch program, and crime in the proscribed area went down some sixty percent.

As does everything, cellular phones have their downside. It is ridiculously easy to eavesdrop on them. All it takes is a few dollars' worth of equipment from Radio Shack and your conversations are in the public domain. So if you're one of those who shop by phone, don't do it by cellular phone because there might be a dozen different bad guys writing down your credit card number.

S I X

AUTOMOBILE SECURITY

Your car is one of the major "where's" of your life. After home and work, the place you spend the most time is in the car. For most people an automobile is much more than just a means of transportation, it is an extension of their ego and makes a personal statement about them. They get behind the wheel, tune into some drumbeat only they can hear, and turn into a starship captain fighting Klingons while circling Uranus.

Before you laugh too loud, remember that a lot of women also go into a different world the second they enter their cars, turning them into mobile music parlors and makeup salons. How many times have you seen it happen or done it yourself? Get in your car, turn on the stereo and interior light, and spend the next five minutes applying various and sundry paints and powders, totally oblivious to the world around. You might as well put up a sign that says, "Abduct me, beat me, rape me, make me write bad checks."

For those of you with children, please do not let the children so occupy your attention that you are not aware of what is happening around you. There have been terrible occurrences where cars have been stolen from unaware mothers with their most precious possession in the backseat. Don't let this terrifying incident happen to you. You must train your older children to get into the car quickly. If you have small infants or toddlers, devise a system for getting your little one and yourself into the car quickly and locking the door before you adjust seat belts and child restraint devices. Most predators take advantage of situations where the potential victim is absorbed with other people and problems.

I'll say it again. Your car is a major part of the "where" of your life. Treat it accordingly.

WALKING TO YOUR CAR

In addition to all the personal things your car may mean to you, it can be a defense against attack, a means of escaping a confrontation, and a deadly weapon in time of need. None of which means a thing if you can't get to it or into it.

Do not stand at the door of your vehicle and spend ten minutes fumbling for your keys. Have them in your hand, ready to insert in the lock before you leave a building to walk to it. Many of today's cars now come with electronic key sets. All you do is press a button and the car either locks or unlocks. If you are in the market for a new car or a late-model used car, buy one with such locks. There is no fumbling for keys. Many electronic keys also turn on the interior lights so that you can see inside the car as you approach it. On my car the backup light also turns on, bathing the car in light.

Be aware of everything around you as you approach the vehicle. I have seen women walking to their car with their heads down, their shoulders stooped, looking at the ground in front of them as if they think they can make themselves really small and the world won't notice them. It sets my nerves on edge. This kind of placid body language sends a clear message to a potential abductor or carjacker that says, "Here I am, take me."

When you walk to your car, stand straight up, hold your head high, and look about. Make sure you see what's going on in the world around you. Throw your shoulders back, suck your stomach in, and put some purpose in your walk. You are not going to escape the notice of anyone who's looking for you, so you might as well walk proudly. By doing so you send a message to a potential abductor that says, "Hey, you may get me, but you're going to pay a price." Reading that message may cause him to hesitate just long enough to let you get inside your vehicle and out of Dodge.

Once inside, do not assume you are safe and therefore free to spend the next five minutes listening to music and painting your face. Your car is a barrier between you and an attack, but it is not an impregnable fortress that will protect you against any and all forms of assault. When you get inside, the very first thing you should do is lock your doors. The second thing is start the engine and fasten seat belts. The third thing is to put the puppy in gear and get out of there, no matter where "there" is. Five seconds after entering the vehicle you should be in motion. ONLY THEN are you fairly safe.

While you are walking to your car, check out the area.

Don't be coy about it, don't worry about someone seeing you do it. If a potential attacker is in the area and watching you, let him know you are on your guard. Take a route that allows you to check out the other side of your car and others immediately around it, making sure no one is hiding behind one of them. If you see someone, flee and call for help. If it turns out to be some guy changing a tire, so what? Blush prettily, bat your eyes, and apologize for any inconvenience you've caused, then tell them you prefer to be safe, not sorry. Check beneath the car and look in the backseat before you enter. Carrying a small flashlight is a good idea.

When you park be sure any valuables are out of sight. This includes packages or suitcases. Put them in the trunk rather than on the backseat. If you own a van, pull the cover over your packages. They're invitations for a passerby to break a window and steal your property. If you know you are going to be parked somewhere after dark, check out the lighting. Make sure you don't leave your vehicle in bright sunlight and have to walk back to it in pitch darkness.

In other words, think ahead and use some common sense. Remember, the best way to survive a confrontation is for the confrontation never to take place. Defend against a confrontation.

CAR CARE

It is important to develop a mind-set that considers your gas tank to be empty when the indicator says half full, and to keep your vehicle in good repair so it is less likely to fail you when you need it most. This is not just for personal security, but also for other emergencies. If you have to take little Johnny to the emergency room at 2:00 in the morning, get stuck in a major freeway traffic jam, or get caught in a bad winter storm, you don't have time to worry about the performance of your car. Keep it full of gas, tuned up, the oil changed, and have good tires. Never, ever take a chance of running out of gas. How many times have you been listening to the radio or watching TV and heard about a missing Jane Doe, only to find out a few days later that she was found naked in a ditch by the side of the road with her car stolen?

Those kinds of stories sicken me, and I'm sure they sicken you as well. Well, how do you think Jane Doe felt when it was happening to her? What do you suppose went through her mind when she knew she was going to be maimed or murdered by some creation out of a horror movie and there wasn't a damn thing she could do about it? How many times did the words "if only" run through her mind? If only I had kept my car in good repair or my gas tank filled so I didn't run out of gas alone on the highway at night. How do you think you will feel if it ever happens to you? Or do you consider yourself one of the chosen few given a card that says "pass go, collect $200"? Are you one of those who just knows it can't happen to them? Well, it can happen to you, and the fact that you are reading this book tells me you are becoming aware of the dangers around you.

MAPS

Learn how to read a map, and keep one in your glove compartment at all times. That way, if you get lost, you don't have to trust to the kindness of strangers for directions. You proceed to a lighted street corner, be sure your doors are locked and you're aware of what's going on around you, then find where you are on the map, where you want to go, and be on your way.

BREAKDOWNS AND ACCIDENTS

In case of a breakdown or an accident, stay in your car if at all possible. This is when you really need the self-defense mechanism called a cellular phone. I understand not everyone can afford one, but you can afford a couple of quarters. If someone comes by to help, roll your window down enough to give out the phone numbers you want called and the required change. Don't get out of the car and start looking under the hood with Joe G. Samaritan, because it may be that not everyone from Samaria has "Good" for a middle name.

If you have to exchange information because of a minor accident it's best to do it from inside. Most states don't require you to get out of your car for any reason, but most people jump out because they want to check the damage. Forget the damage, what's done is done, you can deal with the paperwork later. Above all, listen to your intuition. If you are the least bit uncomfortable don't leave the car. The other person involved can read your driver's license and insurance information through the window. I fully understand it will not always be possible to take these precautions. In a severe accident you may be injured or there may be gas escaping from the tank. There may be other considerations.

If you have to leave your car, use the same good sense you would in a parking lot or anywhere else.

DEALING WITH THE POLICE

If you are alone and signaled to pull over, make sure it is really the police doing the signaling. Police use blue and/or red lights. If an amber light or a white light is flashing, you may have a problem. If you are uncomfortable, even if it is a police officer, ask to move to a better lighted or higher traffic area. We've asked watch commanders and police chiefs all over the country, and they've all said their officers are instructed to do whatever they can to make a woman comfortable. But, as they say in the automobile commercials, your mileage may vary.

Try to understand where the police officer is coming from in these violent days. The guys and gals who work the patrol cars are in a combat zone, and more of their brothers and sisters are hurt or killed during routine traffic stops than anyone likes to remember. Each person wearing a badge must clearly understand they are a single bad judgment away from eternity. Add to that the fact cops have no earthly idea what to expect when they walk up to your car. You may be exactly what you look like, a woman alone who is as scared as they are. On the other hand, you could have three guys with Uzis hiding below the rear window just waiting. It happens all too often and they have to be looking for it.

For that reason, police officers tend to respond to people the way people respond to them. If they walk up to the car and you start screaming at them about how scared you are, or start berating them because they have no business stopping you, or bring them any attitude at all, you are going to make that police officer nervous. One thing you don't want to do in today's world is to make a police officer nervous. Remember, they don't know you from Adam's Uncle Bonzo and they have no reason to trust you, given their experience in life.

If a police officer comes to your car and you are uncomfortable with the location of the event, stay calm, roll your window down enough to talk, and then keep your hands on the wheel in plain sight. Let the officer take charge of the encounter. Do not speak until you are spoken to. If you initiate the conversation, you're taking them out of their script, which means a bell rings inside their head and tells them they aren't in control of the situation. So they begin to get nervous. Don't let that happen.

After the officer initiates the conversation, it's your time to respond. Calmly begin whatever you say with the following words: "Officer, with all due respect . . ." and then say what you want to say. It's dark, you're frightened, could we do this somewhere else, whatever is on your mind. Say it clearly, concisely, and calmly, then shut up and let the officer answer you. If you don't get what you want and want to plead your case further, don't start batting your eyes or sniffling or pleading or raising your voice or giving them grief. Say, "Again, officer, with all due respect . . ." and make your case.

If that still doesn't work and you are still uncomfortable, respectfully ask them to call for another officer or ask to speak with their watch commander. By that time the officer will know you are serious about your discomfort, and something is going to happen, one way or another. Chances are it will be in your favor because the officer is wise enough to know you aren't going through all this aggravation without a reason, and they will have had plenty of time to evaluate you with their own instincts, perhaps even get a report on your license plates.

Let me give you a further word or two of caution. Don't do this if you've been running down the road at twice the speed limit or if you're impaired by alcohol or drugs or if you've been engaging in some other form of stupidity that caused them to pursue you in the first place. Those officers don't care about how much respect you say you have for them, since you've shown you have no respect for them as individuals or the world at large by your actions. Simply another case of the police returning the attitude you have demonstrated.

Keep your common sense close at hand. When asked for your driver's license, since it's probably in your purse, tell them so. Don't just lurch for the purse, grab it, and start fumbling through it. The same goes for your title or insurance forms. When asked for them say, "Officer, my license is in my purse and my insurance certificate is in the glove compartment."

They'll tell you to go ahead, watching you carefully. Do not make a quick move to the glove compartment and reach inside, expecting them to know you're simply going after a piece of paper. You've read the words, "Find the fine and moving line between paranoia and preparedness, then cling to it" twice before in these pages. That's a position police officers must also find. Do not put yourself in a position where your paranoia comes in conflict with theirs. You will lose.

In any situation the most important thing to do is to make sure you're really dealing with an officer. Uniform companies want to sell uniforms and will do so to whoever has money to buy them. Badges can be bought at a pawn shop. Don't forget that police officers are issued municipal, county, or state identification cards by their employer. Ask to see theirs. If you are still uncomfortable, do as suggested above.

Under all situations in dealing with an officer of the law, remember that cops are creatures of instinct. They have their training and their mental procedures just as the rest of us do, but they've seen or heard of too many instances in which instinct prevented injury or death. So they listen carefully to their instincts. If you're a casual speeder, ten miles or so over the speed limit, you're hardly a hardened criminal or a scofflaw. They know that as well as you do.

That is why it is so important to treat them with a certain degree of respect. It does not indicate respect for them as a person, it indicates respect for the society and the body of law they are sworn to protect. If your voice or actions cause them to perceive a negative value judgment of them on your part when all they're doing is their job, they're going to start to wonder why. From that point forward you may be in trouble.

CARJACKING

It may be that the makers of automobile alarms and other protective devices have done their job a bit too well.

Affordable alarm systems and inexpensive items that hold the steering wheel in place have forced criminals to change their operating patterns. Concealed-carry laws in some states have forced them to further adjust their procedures. The combined effect has been to usher us into the era of the carjacker.

In Florida there were several notorious cases of carjackers waiting outside the international flight terminal, choosing foreign tourists, and following them from the car rental areas. The reason for choosing foreign tourists was twofold. Foreigners usually have less familiarity with personal security measures than do Americans, and coming through airport security it's unlikely they would be carrying a firearm. In several cases the tourists were killed. Welcome to the America of the nineties.

I'm not going to spend a lot of time on automobile security devices because there are just too many of them, and most of them work reasonably well. I bought the car that I own because it had a remote locking and unlocking device. When the car is being unlocked, the interior lights also turn on so I can see if there is anyone in the car before getting in. It also includes a noise trigger that can be activated from the same unlocking device. This is particularly helpful in the parking lot situation we discussed earlier.

With all the fancy stuff around, do not forget about your horn. Most of us who live in urban areas are so inured to the sound of auto security alarms, they simply blend into the background noise. Not so with a horn. When you hear long blasts on the horn, you know that someone has to be physically depressing it for it to work, so you pay attention. A honking horn is the automotive equivalent of a screaming pedestrian. When you're afoot, little attracts more attention than a scream; in your car, little attracts more attention than a continuously blowing horn.

Carjackings, like most crimes, usually take place in ways convenient to the criminal. The primary locations are self-service gas pumps, stoplights, traffic jams, or intentional accidents, usually minor fender-benders.

Always make sure that when and where you get your gas is your choice. It was mentioned above to never let your car get less than half full. This is one of the reasons why. You don't need to find yourself at 3:00 A.M. in an area of town you don't know with two teaspoons of gasoline left to get you home. Remember, it's easy for people to get in your car while you're getting gas if you leave your doors open or unlocked. So take the keys with you and lock the door. There are many stations with ATM-style devices for credit card payment right at the pump and you never have to leave your car. However, while you're getting the nozzle or pumping gas, it takes only two seconds for a thief to get in your car and be gone, leaving you standing there watching your car tooling down the road. So take the keys out of the car, and for even greater security, lock the car while pumping gas or paying the attendant.

You might consider getting a lock for your gas tank while you're at it. There is one out now that is a combination lock, and inside the cap is a place where you can secrete an extra key and a few dollars that a thief may not be able to retrieve. The lock is a good idea for another reason. If your car is hijacked at a gas station, the reason you're there is because you need gas. There is a chance the thief will run out of gas and have to abandon your car before he gets it to the chop shop to be broken up and sold piece by piece at "Parts R Us Emporium."

One little piece of good sense most of us forget from time to time is to lock our doors as we zoom down the road, preferably with the windows raised. The doors on my vehicle automatically lock when I turn on the ignition. I understand that not everyone has air conditioning, and it's fun to feel the breeze in your face on nice days, but you need to remember you're vulnerable when you do so.

Law enforcement personnel disagree on which lane is best to use when you have to stop at a sign or a light. Some say use the right lane. If someone attacks you when you're in the right lane, you can make an immediate right turn. In most places that's not even illegal. If the traffic is too heavy to turn, there is always the sidewalk, assuming you can use it without harming a pedestrian.

Another group says to use the center lane. The reason is that the nearer you are to the curb, the more convenient it is for a carjacker to make his move. If you're in the center lane he has to walk through oncoming traffic and has more distance to cover, giving you more time to see him and get away.

One thing both sides agree on is never to stop anywhere without leaving a full length between you and the car in front. That way you have some wiggle room if something happens. Otherwise you're simply locked in traffic with no place to go.

Remember the rules of dealing with an accident in case

one happens, and keep those doors locked. It may be a car-jacking or an insurance scam. What usually happens is that one driver will be in a crash car and will engineer a way to stop you, perhaps slamming on his brakes in front of you so you run into his rear end. You know you're in trouble because you've heard from day one that if you rear-end someone it's always your fault. Therefore, you get out to plead your case, exchange information, or simply vent. Meanwhile, unseen by you, a car stops behind you, a passenger gets out and takes off down the road in your car.

However, if an armed carjacker approaches you and you cannot drive away, you have a very difficult decision. If you get out and give him the car keys, will he take the car and *only* leave you stranded, or could you possibly become a victim of physical abuse? This is one situation in which your instincts might be your best ally.

SEVEN

PHYSICAL SECURITY

Your best weapons and most loyal allies in seeing to your personal security are your instincts. Heed them.

Most of us are far more instinctive than we realize. When you choose a melon at the market, you look at several and finally choose one. Why? You're not a farmer, what do you know about melons? Why not simply pick the first one you see? You meet someone new, introduced to you by a friend. You take an instant dislike to the person, no reason. They looked right, dressed right, said all the right words, but for some reason you can't put your finger on you don't like the person. Someone else dresses like something out of a bad movie and says none of the right words, yet you like them. Some little voice tells you this person is worth something.

Those are your instincts speaking to you. They may be right or wrong, no one says they have to be perfect. But there's one significant thing about them you should remember. Your instincts are the only thing on earth that has your personal survival as their sole reason for existing. Never forget it and never fail to listen to them. They're like a muscle, the more you exercise them, the more you use them, the more important you let them become in your life, the more acute and accurate they become.

For instance, if someone stops you and asks you for the time but maybe he or she doesn't feel right, gets a little too close, or is overly aggressive, that little bell goes off in your head or your stomach and says, "This isn't right!" Don't start to intellectualize or rationalize. Just get away. Don't worry about hurting someone else's feelings, don't worry about embarrassment, just get away. Remember the earlier story about the shepherd boy who cried wolf. The wolf was always there, he just jumped back into the bushes when the villagers came. The first time the villagers stayed home, the wolf ate lamb chops and the boy.

You walk up to your door, open it, something doesn't feel right. Get away from there. You have an instinct that tells you don't go there, don't do this; then don't go there or do that. Listen to it.

I believe if you are attuned to your instincts and act on them you'll save yourself all sorts of misery, and not just the kind caused by physical harm. How many times have you heard someone say, "I knew I shouldn't have done that," after something negative has happened? When I hear that, I just want to grab the person and shake him or her and say, "If you knew you shouldn't have done it, why in the name of reason and sanity did you do it?"

Unfortunately, you can have the best instincts in the world and render them totally useless. It's not hard. All you have to do is ignore them.

Follow your instincts. It cannot be said often enough. Follow your instincts as if your life depended on doing so. The day may come when it does.

HOW TO USE YOUR INSTINCTS

One of the primary instincts, an involuntary reaction to being attacked, is to scream. Some people in law enforcement think it's a bad idea, others think it's a good idea. Personally, I think it's a very good idea. If you're walking along somewhere, anywhere, and a bad guy comes out of the woods and pounces on you, scream your ever loving head off. Scream and keep on screaming. Don't stop until he's gone. There is a big exception to this rule: if he is threatening you with a weapon and he demands that you stop. In all other circumstances, scream as if your life depended on it.

Screaming may be your best protection when you're in areas that make you feel vulnerable. We find that some of the places where women feel most vulnerable alone in public are the mall, grocery stores, or the bank—locations where someone has more or less a clear shot at you or your purse. One thing to do is visualize the place where you are going and imagine how you might react if something happened.

We all use ATMs these days. Try locating one that is inside a building, rather than on a dark and deserted street. Many grocery stores have them, big stores like Wal-Mart or Kmart have them. Avoid using outside machines if at all possible. If you must use one, check it out the same way you would a self-service gas station or a dark parking lot. Drive-through ATMs are a little better. Predators know that when you go to an ATM, the only reason you're there is to get money, so be on your guard each and every time you use one. ATMs are all over the place. If the first one you come to looks uninviting and scary, find another one.

Parking garages are another spot where people feel particularly vulnerable. The stairwells in them are frequently cramped and poorly lit, so law enforcement agencies even suggest that parkers walk up or down the ramps instead of using the stairs. Obviously, you have to be extremely careful of traffic, but in case someone puts a move on you there is room to maneuver.

When walking with packages, always try to keep one hand free. If you're walking to your car, you have your keys in one hand, your packages in the other. If you are right-handed, carry the packages in your left hand and have your keys ready. If someone does try something, drop the packages and get out of there. Your keys are in your hand, so jump in the car and go.

When you are walking down the street, keep an eye to the reflections in the glass windows. They can be used exactly like a mirror. Check them out from time to time. If your instincts are telling you there is a problem nearby, window reflections are a good way to check around without being obvious.

Use the rearview mirror in your car the same way. If you think you are being followed, make a turn or two and see if you are correct. If the car you're suspicious of stays with you and you have a cellular phone, call the police and tell them what's going on. If you don't have a phone, pull into a police station and file a report. If there is no police station in the area, head into a very public place, maybe a grocery store parking lot, pull up next to the door and get inside, then make the reporting call.

Do not drive straight home and try to get inside before the person can grab you. You may not make it. And all you're doing is leading someone who wants to steal from you or do you physical harm straight to your door. In many cases, this is exactly what the criminal wants you to do. Police in many different states have reported numerous instances of people pulling into their driveways only to find a predator behind them, barring them from getting away. They are then robbed and often killed.

If you are going home and believe that you are being followed, drive right by your home and then drive to the police station. You say you don't know where the nearest police station to your house is? Please go and find it right now. And while you are looking, find the fire station and fire hydrant.

ELEVATORS

Elevators are particularly threatening. When waiting for the elevator, stand away from the doors. This keeps anyone who might already be on the elevator from grabbing you and pulling you in. It also gives you a second to evaluate whoever else is on it and make sure that the occupants are people with whom you want to share a confined space. Do the same thing when you're inside the elevator and want to get out. Stand back so you can evaluate the situation in the lobby in case you might suddenly decide to change your mind about getting off.

If you get on the elevator and suddenly feel you shouldn't have—perhaps someone's hands "accidentally" brush against where they shouldn't—get back off before the doors close. Don't worry about what anyone else around thinks. You don't owe them an explanation for your actions and there is no reason you should care what they think about anything. If the doors have closed, hit the next floor button and get off as soon as possible.

When you do get on an elevator, if at all possible stand next to the control panel so you're in charge of where the car goes. Take clear note of what is on the panel, because on most of them you'll find both the "stop" and "alarm" button are both red. If something happens and you punch the wrong red button, instead of a bell ringing the car stops. Then the guy's got you where he wants you. Bad news. Know the lay of the land, no matter where you are, even if the land you're dealing with is fifteen square feet of elevator car.

PEDESTRIAN ACTIVITIES

No matter how many people are around, when you're walking or jogging you are truly alone. Your support staff, family, friends, coworkers, and others are elsewhere. To coin a phrase, there's never a cop around when you need one and only fools and dead playwrights depend on the kindness of strangers. When you're on the street by yourself, you have to be ready to take care of business.

Always walk in the opposite direction of traffic, even if you're walking on the sidewalk. There are a couple of reasons. First, it's more difficult to abduct someone off the street if they're moving in the opposite direction of the abductor's vehicle. The simple physics of bodies moving in opposite directions works for you. The other thing is, if a car coming toward you loses control or there is an accident, you have a chance to get out of the way because you can see it. If the car is coming from behind and there is no unusual noise to alert you, an out-of-control vehicle stands an excellent chance of turning you into roadkill.

If someone stops and asks for information or directions, do not walk up to their car, lean into the window, and talk to them like they're old friends. Stand back from the car, well out of arms' length, and answer their questions. If you have an instinct (there's that word again) screaming that there is something wrong with this picture, get out of there. Don't wait to think about it, don't worry about hurting the feelings of some poor lost tourist, just beat feet.

Give blind spots, recessed doorways, alleys, or large shrubs a wide berth. If someone is hiding in or behind one of the above waiting for you, be sure they have to take a few steps and make a dedicated effort to get to you. The few extra seconds it takes them to reach you gives you needed time to react, and may literally be the difference between life and death.

Evaluate the situation on the outside when leaving a building. If there is normally exterior lighting and the light is out, go back inside and find out why. If there's a group of teenagers or anything else that might be intimidating outside, go back in and see if there is a security guard to walk you to your car. If there is no security guard, go find a male in one of the offices and ask him to walk with you to your car. I fully understand that this may cost you a bit of pride, but pride is renewable. Dead is forever.

Always carry a flashlight. With all the junk most of us carry in our purses, you'll never know it's there until you need it. Small intensity lights are available, just a few inches long and an inch or so in diameter, that give immense amounts of light for their size.

JOGGING

If you're a jogger and you just have to run in the parks or on the street rather than in the relative safety of your club's track, be especially careful. Joggers usually like to run the same path at the same time of day. This is a pattern that's easily noticeable by a criminal, so you must take extra care. Leave your Walkman at home, you need all your senses acutely attuned to the world around you, and that includes the sense of sound. The more you isolate yourself from your surroundings, the more you place yourself at risk.

Remember that a large portion of being secure is to

remove the impression of vulnerability; we discussed this in the home security section. We also discussed presenting an illusion of invulnerability. At this writing, thirty-one states have passed laws requiring them to issue citizens' permits to carry concealed firearms if the citizen meets certain criteria. To accommodate the increasing demand for firearm-concealing devices, a manufacturer has come out with a fanny-pack that is actually a holster. Instead of wearing it in back, wear it on the left side of your stomach, if you're right-handed. If a bad guy has been watching you, he may recognize the pack as a holster. Think, you've just received your carry license and are now armed. Do not forget and leave it at home once you start wearing it, because on the off chance someone has been clocking you, that will tell them you've forgotten your gun and are vulnerable.

Remember that criminals are sight feeders. They're like a bass in a lake, they see something they like, think they want it at a given moment in time, they snap at it on reflex. Remember this when you put on your tank top and short skirt or that exercise outfit that fits like a second skin. I'm not going to tell you how or how not to dress, or pass any judgments on what you wear. Violence against women has as much to do with asserting power as it does with sex, but you absolutely *must* understand that your actions can affect someone else—that's the world we live in. If you're sashaying along in revealing clothes and a latter-day Ted Bundy or even a simpleminded rapist drives by, you could be in a world of trouble. That type of person doesn't care about your right to wear whatever you want and do whatever you want, because as far as he's concerned concepts of right and wrong don't apply to him. His solitary interest is sating whatever fleeting whim passes through his mind. Try not to become his whim.

PURSES

Do you really need all that junk in your purse? The first thing to do in making your purse secure is to take everything out that's not absolutely necessary to what you're doing at a given time. Once you've done that, spread your important documents around. By that I mean spread them around on your body, not your purse. Put your driver's license in one pocket, a little money and your credit cards in other pockets, and so on. That way, if someone does manage to separate you from your purse, they don't take your entire life with them.

Law enforcement is of two minds as to how one should carry a purse. Some say carry it with the strap over your head and shoulder, others say just on your shoulder with a hand on it, to let the world know you know it's there. I favor the on-the-shoulder approach. If someone grabs it and runs, you have the opportunity to grab back and give it one good tug. If that doesn't work, let it go. If it's around your neck, you stand a chance of being pulled off your feet and breaking bones, being dragged along, or pulled into the grasp of your attacker. The object is to keep as much distance between you and the criminal as possible. You don't want to be tied to him so he can beat you half to death while stealing the few bucks you're carrying.

Don't ever just stand there and fight anyone for it. If

you're in a tug of war for your purse, throw it away. Throw it as far as you can and then run in the opposite direction. A purse snatcher is after money. His primary intention is not to hurt you. By throwing your purse you separate yourself from his objective. Nine times out of ten he'll go for the purse, giving you the time you need to get away.

EIGHT

THE REALITY OF UNARMED SELF-DEFENSE

On the subject of unarmed self-defense, there is one point which I can't make strongly enough: YOU DON'T WANT TO DO IT! I don't mean that you shouldn't consider studying unarmed self-defense techniques and incorporating them into your overall personal safety strategy, because you should. And I absolutely don't mean that you should not be prepared to defend yourself with whatever is necessary —fists, feet, elbows, knees, teeth, or whatever—because you should.

What I do mean is that AVOIDING a fight is ALWAYS the best strategy, and that's why the rest of this book is about staying safe through avoiding criminal attack. I emphasize avoidance because the grim reality is that if you are forced to physically defend yourself against an attacker, even if you survive, you are very likely to be hurt! Here's why:

Most law-abiding citizens, especially women, have very little fighting experience. You may not have been in a fight since a kindergarten hair-pulling contest, and I suspect you're not out there now starting barroom brawls! One of the many reasons we ARE law-abiding is that we share the basic value that fighting is, at best, a last resort in resolving conflict and then only in self-defense. Your attacker, on the other hand, lives violence every day. It's the way he makes a living. When confronted with such an attacker, you will have to overcome your natural aversion to violence in order to survive. Your attacker doesn't have this problem.

Your attacker believes he is capable of harming you, so he has yet another psychological edge. Common sense tells us that most people only start fights they think they can win. In the case of criminal attack this is absolutely true, because career criminals only prey on those whom they consider to be easy targets. As we have discussed, this does not necessarily mean small or weak-looking people. Criminals look for someone they believe they can attack without being hurt themselves, usually someone who is unaware of their surroundings, preoccupied with something, or naively feels secure. Remember: Find that thin, moving line between paranoia and preparedness and cling to it.

You will be fighting on his terms. He picks the time and place to attack you to his best advantage. Awareness and preparedness are your only defenses against this.

You are outmatched. Career criminals are experienced and often instinctual fighters. Criminals learn hand-to-hand fighting in the toughest possible training environment: prison. Your attacker has probably been in and out of jail several times. In jail, he has had to literally fight for his life, and since he is attacking you, you know he survived prison. Career criminals also practice fighting skills in prison. They practice how to quickly and seriously hurt you, how to disarm you, and how to use their own weapons.

The longer you fight, the greater your chances are of being injured or killed.

So the odds are stacked against you. At this point, you may ask, "Well, if I can't avoid a fight, how can I possibly win, Tanya?"

Let's talk about "winning" for a moment. In a fight, what does it mean to win?

Well, forget about John Wayne, Rocky Balboa, or Jean-Claude Van Damme. For all of the reasons mentioned, you won't be able to take out one bad guy, let alone a roomful. And it's not your job to play cop and catch the bad guy either. Experienced martial artists know that, in a street fight, they will fight at twenty-five to fifty percent of their normal, unstressed, practice ability. Think about what this means for those of us who aren't martial arts experts!

The situation is not hopeless, however. We just need to reconsider what winning a fight means. It does not mean annihilating your attacker. For you, me, and the rest of the law-abiding citizenry, winning a fight means escaping it alive! If you are alive at the end of a fight, you win. You stay alive by keeping the fight short and escaping it as quickly as possible.

And this leads us to my basic, unarmed, self-defense strategy:

INFLICT PAIN. DETER ATTACK. ESCAPE!

If escape is not immediately an option and you are forced to defend yourself, you must INFLICT PAIN on your attacker. This will get his attention and, hopefully, make him reconsider his decision to attack you. Remember, criminals don't want to get hurt either on the streets. As in nature, injured predators become prey themselves.

By successfully inflicting pain, you will DETER further ATTACK. You may even make your attacker completely break off his assault and go looking for easier pickings. At worst, the pain you cause your attacker should buy you a couple of precious seconds.

Once the attack has been deterred, you must ESCAPE immediately! Otherwise, your attacker will just resume his efforts and you will still be in danger. Run as fast as you can, scream, use that cellular phone, get in your car, and find someone you can trust to help you. If you are injured, get to a hospital. Finally, try to remember how your attacker looked, acted, smelled, and sounded. This will be valuable information for the police.

Before we go into the various fighting arts you can study, I want to make you aware of two other self-defense realities. Each one of us is always armed; and no one, no matter how big and tough, is invulnerable.

Always armed? "Tanya, I don't carry a gun or knife," you say. No, but you are armed. Your body is full of self-defense tools. Your fingers, fingernails, fists, hands, elbows, teeth, skull, knees, and feet can all be used to inflict pain on an attacker. And all of us, even the bad guys, have generally the same vulnerable areas: eyes, nose, mouth, ears, throat, hands, nipples, sternum, solar plexus, floating ribs, groin, knees, shins, and feet. If you are forced to fight, your natural self-defense tools can be used against your attacker's vulnerable areas to cause him considerable pain.

The challenge is learning how to effectively and efficiently use your natural self-defense tools, and this is where studying one of the many fighting arts can be of value. There is no ultimate fighting art that will make you unbeatable, but studying a martial art that is practical, geared toward self-defense, and fits your needs can make the difference in your ability to survive an attack.

Throughout history, in all parts of the world, for personal as well as national defense, people have developed and practiced techniques to make them better fighters. Most martial arts systems are designed to give the smaller, weaker fighter the advantage through skill and technique.

To help you understand your many choices in martial arts styles, I'm going to categorize them by the type of techniques they use. I break martial arts systems down into four basic groups: punching/kicking, grappling, internal, and self-defense systems. Almost all martial arts styles incorporate some elements from all four groups, but most systems emphasize one type of technique over the others.

The punching/kicking styles work just the way you would think. They rely upon punches and kicks to survive a fight. Some styles of punching/kicking you will find are: boxing, jeet kune do, karate, kick-boxing, kung fu, savate, tae kwon do, tang soo do, wing chun, and various other southeast Asian arts too numerous to name. As you can see from this list, one advantage of the kicking/punching systems is that they are numerous and widely available. A potential disadvantage for some women is that many rely upon speed and strength for their effectiveness and require a high degree of physical fitness from the student.

The grappling systems are based upon holds, joint locks, pressure points, and throws. Also fairly common, some grappling systems are aikido, aikijutsu, hapkido, judo, jujitsu, sumo, and wrestling.

Whatever martial art you choose, I think every woman should learn some grappling skills. They are important because very few real fights are merely an exchange of punches and kicks like the ones we see in the movies and on TV. Most street fights end up with the combatants wrestling on the ground, and this is especially true in the case of attacks against women, so here is where grappling skills can save your bacon.

By the same token, you don't want to get that up close and personal with an attacker if you can avoid it. So be careful that your self-defense skills are not limited only to grappling techniques that require you to wrestle with your attacker.

The basis of internal systems is a little harder to grasp, especially for Americans. Some examples are chi kung, tai chi chuan, hsing-I, and pa-kua. They are called "internal" systems because they strive to create internal strength or energy, something called "chi" or "ki" by their practitioners. These arts are studied and enjoyed by many Americans of all ages, and watching someone practice an internal style, tai chi chuan for example, is like seeing a very slow, graceful, and deliberate dance (which is actually a series of martial arts moves). I would not make an internal system my first choice when looking for a self-defense fighting art, but many martial artists study an internal art in addition to one of the other systems, because they are especially good for developing stamina, balance, and control.

The self-defense arts are systems that focus exclusively on techniques for use against a violent attacker, and I divide the self-defense classes into two common types. The first is the basic introductory type. Often lasting just a few lessons, perhaps being taught in a community education center, an introductory self-defense class usually provides a woman with some basic techniques for use against an attacker. For a beginner, these may be worth considering because they usually don't require a big investment in time or money, and they can give you an idea about what types of fighting techniques work best for you.

The other type of self-defense course is a women-only, full-contact class. These classes also provide an introduction to basic techniques, but allow the students to practice in the classroom against a mock attacker who is wearing full-body, soft, protective armor. The armor allows you to punch, kick, elbow, knee, and gouge the mock attacker as hard as you can—as hard as you would need to in a real fight. I like these courses because you come about as close to a real street fight as you ever want to get. This experience can be a life saver, because if you are attacked and need to defend yourself, you have at least done something like it before. A martial art, however, as with any skill, requires continuing practice to be effective, so I recommend that you view self-defense classes as a good starting point.

Good places to start looking for a martial arts school are the Yellow Pages under "karate" or in a catalog of classes at your local YMCA or community college. Contact your police department for their recommendation. The following is a laundry list of questions to which you want answers before you lay down your money and invest your time in a martial arts school.

What kind of martial art is it? Do the classes integrate other personal protection and avoidance skills with the martial arts techniques? Do they teach you to inflict pain to deter attack in order to escape? What is the school's emphasis? Tournament competition, self-defense, traditional? This last question requires some explanation. Many schools train students to compete in tournaments, and others train them in a culturally traditional manner. Both of these approaches are fine, but if the school's emphasis is not primarily self-defense, you need to consider if their approach will give you the survival skills you are seeking.

How long has the school been in business? Ask neighboring businesses what they think of the school, its owner, and its students. How many students does it have? How many are women? Are there women instructors? When are the classes held and for how long? What system or association provided the chief instructor with his or her credentials? How much instruction is from the chief instructor and how much from other students?

What is the cost per lesson? Do you have to prepay for a certain number of lessons? Is there a refund if you have to or want to quit? Are there additional charges? Can you watch one of the classes? Can you talk with some of the students? Are there any students like you (similar age, sex, build) with whom you can speak? Get the opinion of a student with whom you can identify. If you are a five-foot-two, 110-pound woman, the comments of a six-foot-four, 225-pound male may not give you the information you need. If there are no students like you, this might tell you something!

You probably won't get perfect answers to all of these questions, but they are important to you as a women and as a consumer. Before you make a decision, get as many answers as possible, preferably from several martial arts schools, and make the best decision you can. If you have a bad feeling about a particular school, that's a good reason to avoid it. Studying a martial art can involve a serious commitment of time and money. Most important, as a part of your overall personal protection strategy, one day you may have to depend on what you learned. Choose wisely.

As I have said, no martial art is going to turn you into superwoman. The greatest advantage of studying a fighting art is that it forces you to think about your own personal defense on a regular basis. This enhanced awareness, combined with your fighting skills, can make a crucial difference in surviving a criminal attack. An important secondary benefit is that regular practice of martial arts is excellent exercise, not unlike aerobics, and it can help to keep you in good physical shape.

Once again, above all, strive to avoid criminal attack. Find that thin, moving line between paranoia and preparedness and cling to it. If you can't avoid a fight, remember that winning a fight means escaping it alive! If you are alive at the end of a fight, you win. You stay alive by keeping the fight short and escaping it as quickly as possible. Remember: Inflict pain to deter further attack and escape to safety.

NINE

PERSONAL
PROTECTION DEVICES

Most rational, noncriminal members of society do not want to seriously injure, maim, or kill another human being. Therefore, many forms of nonlethal self-defense weapons have been invented. And as has been stated previously, the first line of self-defense is to stay out of or get out of a bad situation. To get out, the intended victim must have a way of convincing the attacker that he may meet some resistance. After all, criminals are just like electricity, they take the path of least resistance.

Most personal protection devices are always dangerous and can be deadly. If you're going to use one or more of the items discussed in this section, you should also be aware that laws vary from state to state, often with little rhyme or reason. What's legal in your jurisdiction may not be legal just across the state or county line. An old saw says, "Ignorance is no excuse in the eyes of the law." It's never truer than in the case of things like sprays and pain compliance devices, as their use runs the gamut from totally unrestricted to a felony depending on the geography.

You must be responsible for these items at all times. For instance, you don't want to leave a can of pepper spray lying around so the baby can find it and accidentally spray him- or herself. When you buy something for self-defense, you must understand how and why it works, practice with it, and make its use second nature. When it comes time to use these devices, you will have only a split second, and you don't want to wait until then to read the instructions.

The key is presence of mind. You must know—not think, not believe, not hope—but KNOW! exactly how you're going to use your chosen device when the time comes. That means having familiarity with the weapon, and practice, Practice, PRACTICE! If you are not willing to make such a commitment, don't bother buying any of these devices.

STUN GUNS

Stun guns are nonlethal weapons that have the possibility of deterring a would-be attacker. In theory, a stun gun emits electrical shocks that can run up to 200,000 volts. The shock is so dramatic to the body that it overloads the neural and muscular system. So many different messages are sent to the brain at the same time, there aren't enough paths for them to get there, so the body begins to shut down. The stun gun does not affect the heart. If properly used, it acts on local muscle tissue, which starts contracting, resulting in loss of muscle control.

There are several types of stun guns. They have varying strengths; some emit a pulse charge, others send a constant charge. The constant charge is supposed to be a little better, as it is said to affect an attacker more quickly. All of them have two types of probes, test probes and contact probes. The test probes are the two obvious extensions at the end that allow you to check out the machine. If your battery is in good working order, when you test it you'll see a blue line of electricity. If you don't see the static line, change the battery.

The actual voltage of the stun gun is important. I have seen stun guns for sale for less than $20. Don't buy them. If you are going to own and carry a stun gun, buy one that has at least the capability of delivering 100,000 volts. In addition, make sure that your batteries are fresh. The voltage the stun gun delivers is only as good as the battery that is powering it.

The test probes, besides allowing the owner to check out the battery, can be used to deter an attacker. If someone is menacing you, pulling out and energizing your stun gun may deter him. The crackling noise and the blue flame can cause an attacker to think twice. Remember, most criminals do not want to get into an altercation, so a noisy blue electric charge can become a deterrent.

The actual contact probes that deliver the electricity are farther down on the device, which means that in order to deliver the electric charge you have to hold it against an attacker for some length of time, usually around four seconds. In plain English, you don't just touch someone, punch the zap button, and have them hit the floor. It is important to know where to put those probes. They must be near bone or muscle. The sternum or chest is probably the best place. The bones of the chest will carry the electrical current into the neuromuscular system. Other parts that work well are the throat, armpits, or hip joints. An arm or an attacker's stomach may not work at all.

Now, I am not sure that I want to stand next to a potential rapist who is six inches taller than I am and weighs at least fifty more pounds for three to four seconds. Remember, the charge has to get through to the muscle, and the device can be hindered by clothing. This might not be a problem if you live in South Florida, but in Chicago it might be.

There's another type out called a taser, which shoots two prongs that attach to the attacker and transmit the charge by wire. The benefit is that you can use them from a distance; but the barbs have to be aimed, have to hit, have to pierce the clothing—and once all that has happened you're attached to your attacker by a wire.

ALARMS

It appears that noisemakers are being sold in every type of shop, from the local convenience store to the upscale electronics gadgetry market in your local mall. Noise is a deterrent because most criminals don't want the whole world watching what they are doing. But I don't think much of alarms as personal security devices. Someone in the crowd may call for help if one goes off, but don't count on it. My daughter lives in New York City, and when I visit her I am always astonished by the number of car alarms that are being set off and no one pays any attention.

If you do use an alarm, remember that it requires batteries. Be sure the batteries are always fresh. You don't want to find yourself in a position where you have to use the thing and nothing happens when you pull the plug.

First of all, make sure the noisemaking gadget is loud. The lowest decibel level should be about 110dB. Also, be sure that it doesn't sound like a car alarm. Too many people are inured to the sound of car alarms; they don't even pause to look around. I have seen and heard well-meaning police officers suggest whistles to elderly ladies. Please get something noisier than a whistle. There are devices on the market which activate an ear-piercing noise when you blow into them.

There is one that has a pin-pull activator. The alarm fits in your purse. Around your wrist is a cord attached to the alarm's pin. When someone grabs your purse, the pin is pulled out and the alarm sounds. There is another alarm made specifically for joggers. It's carried in your hand, similar to walking weights. It activates when it's squeezed. Studies have shown that when people are frightened or stressed they tend to clench their fists, so this one is designed to take advantage of that response. If someone jumps out of the bushes, you may scream and clench your fist, and the alarm goes off.

Personal alarms are most effective in crowds, where sound alone may be a deterrent to criminal activity. They may be effective against purse snatching and other forms of small-time crime. I would not suggest you depend on them to dissuade a determined attacker.

CHEMICAL AND PEPPER SPRAYS

There are a number of different chemical sprays on the market, though many state legislatures have begun to legislate against their use by other than police and military. The chemical sprays go by many different names, such as Mace, Paralyzer, Phaser, and others. They work by spraying a constricted stream that begins to evaporate once it comes into contact with a person's skin, releasing chemical vapors that then sting or irritate the skin and the mucous membranes of the eyes, nose, and throat, and mouth.

It has been found that chemical sprays have less of a deterrent effect against persons under the influence of alcohol or drugs, or those who have severe psychological problems. They also are not very effective against animal attack. Law enforcement agencies in many areas have been phasing out the use of Mace in favor of pepper spray, so that should tell you something.

Pepper sprays, on the other hand, are effective against both animals and humans who are under the influence of outside chemical factors. The pepper in pepper spray is just that—oil of pepper, which goes by the Latin name of Oleoresin Capsicum. But all you really need to know is that one drop of the alkaloid it's made from is noticeable in 100,000 drops of water. These sprays cause instant and intense burning pain, major constriction of the throat leading to difficulty in breathing, acute nausea leading to involuntary vomiting, and if hit in the eyes, instant though not permanent blindness.

Most pepper sprays are delivered in a mist, not a stream

like chemical sprays. For most people, aiming a mist is infinitely easier than aiming a stream. However, it should be noted that a mist affects anyone within the three- to four-foot range. Many manufacturers claim a longer range, but unless a strong wind is at your back, stick with three to four feet. If you see a pepper foam, pass it by. Foam doesn't work. Some pepper sprays are delivered in a fog. A fogger has the capability of delivering up to twenty feet away. However, the fog will debilitate everyone with whom it comes into contact, including the sprayer, and it should never be used inside or where there are innocent people around. The most effective delivery system is the modified stream. The range is six to eight feet and is less affected by wind than the mist.

When you buy pepper spray or Mace, remember to check out the canister design. They come in all sorts of containers. Some can fit on a key chain, look like a gun or ball point pen, or exist as a hand sprayer. In many areas some of them are considered to be a concealed weapon, so consult your state and local laws before dropping one in your purse.

The container, which can range from a half-ounce size to a three-pound size, includes the aluminum can itself, the inside tube, a nozzle, a nozzle cover, and a seal. The inside tube is usually a thin plastic pipe. The type of spray and the distance it can travel are determined by the kind of nozzle used. The nozzle cover is usually a plastic covering that operates the nozzle, keeps it clean, and on some cans can have an on/off switch. The seal ensures that the mixture inside the aerosol can stays there until it is needed. Since most containers use some kind of gas propellant, it is very important that the seal be made of Teflon rather than rubber.

The shelf life of most propellants is one to two years. Nitrogen has a longer shelf life, two to three years. When buying pepper spray, you can never tell how long it has been since the container was originally filled. It is commonly believed that the smaller the container, the shorter the shelf life. Small cans have a one- to two-year shelf life, while large cans, more than two ounces, are good for one year. Check out the can. Is there any sign of leakage? Red stains on the can, a pepper smell from the nozzle? Is the packaging labeling on straight and does it look like a quality product? Buy from a reputable store and ask about shelf life. A legitimate manufacturer and store will readily replace a bad unit. A container of pepper spray is absolutely useless unless the pepper is delivered to the attacker.

In order to deliver the spray, the pepper is mixed with liquid. It is important to know what kind of liquid is used. Do not buy a can that includes alcohol or any flammable product. Some pepper sprays have been found to contain toxic materials. There is currently legal action in California against a pepper spray manufacturer whose product may have caused some deaths. As with everything you buy, read the label.

Now for the basic ingredient, pepper. Nearly everyone gets their pepper from the same source. The question is, how much pepper should actually be in the can ready to be delivered to your attacker. The heat range of the substance is measured in Scoville heat units. They range from about 5,000 units for a Bell pepper up to 2,000,000 for a Habanero. When you buy pepper spray, check to see how hot it is. You're looking for a minimum of 100,000 Scoville heat units. At that number or above you can cause whomever you spray some significant misery.

Also check out the strength of the solution. You want something that has no less than eight percent oil versus carrier. The carrier is the solution that carries the agent to the bad guy's face, the oil is what does the damage once it gets there. Most states won't sell more than a ten-percent solution to civilians. If you live in California and go jogging where mountain lions range, you may want the strongest spray you can find. And by the way, all pepper spray is orange/red because of the color of the oil.

Pepper spray can be very effective, properly used. Just remember that, like all such devices, using it requires training. Pepper spray doesn't require much, but you have to know how to get it ready for action and which direction to point it. You must be aware of how long you've had a particular canister, because it uses an aerosol propellant and will lose pressure over time. You don't want to whip it out and punch the button and have it spurt instead of spray. If you're going to use pepper spray, make sure you know what you are doing and that your equipment works.

All these deterrent devices give you the time to try to get away from your attacker. If you use pepper spray, or if you choose to use a stun gun or a taser, remember that once the device has been activated, don't stay around to see what happens. Get away as fast as possible and don't look back.

Make sure you learn how to use your device, know its limitations, and practice, practice, practice. It is your life we are talking about.

TEN

SELF-DEFENSE: YOUR PRIMARY CIVIL RIGHT

While I was involved in developing the Refuse To Be A Victim program, I had the opportunity to talk with many women. They were diverse geographically, ethnically, and in age. Although there were a few pacifists, most of them would agree that they had a right and a duty to defend themselves from the criminal predator. In fact, even most of the pacifists would vehemently agree that they would defend their children even if they did not believe in self-defense. Most women want to believe that they live in safe neighborhoods and that predators are after the other guy.

Fortunately, when the question is pressed, they really do recognize that we live in perilous times and that the streets and byways of our towns and cities can be and are fraught with danger. It is unfortunate that humankind still has not eradicated the plague of criminals and predators, but history is full of perils. Today it may be the carjacker or the drug dealer, but each era in history has had perils peculiar to its time. Only the nature of the danger changes; the presence of peril is eternal.

Prehistoric humans faced bears and saber-toothed tigers with long teeth and sharp claws. Our ancestors were severely hampered by their relatively smaller size and lack of equivalent teeth. So some caveman or woman got the idea of sharpening the end of a stick and when the bear charged our ancestor, maybe the bear was deterred by a sharp jab. Later on someone else got the idea of tying a sharpened rock on the end of a smaller stick and using another stick and a piece of vine to propel it into the bear from a distance. Suddenly bears and tigers weren't quite the threat they used to be. I am sure bears and tigers still made meals of two-legged creatures but at least some of our ancestors had a fighting chance.

Henry V's archers used the longbow so effectively at Agincourt that tens of thousands of Frenchmen were killed during that battle with almost no loss to the British. Crowned heads trembled all over Europe, worrying that with such a weapon the English could rule the world. A few moments passed, they got over their fear and started making longbows of their own. Suddenly the English weren't quite as frightening.

Someone once told Napoleon that he prayed for God to be on their side in the coming battle. Napoleon replied, "God is on the side with the heaviest artillery." The Russians proved the statement all over again in World War II. The

Germans on the Russian Front were much better trained and equipped. The Russians bided their time, let winter take its toll, then brought out the artillery and pounded on the Germans until they withdrew. Again, the big guns won the day.

Potential victims who have the wherewithal to defend themselves are winning the day in the fight against crime, as well. According to Dr. Gary Kleck of Florida State University, who has studied self-defensive use of firearms in two highly acclaimed studies, the availability of a firearm gives the individual, even if the potential victim is a female, a fighting chance. Dr. Kleck's analysis of National Crime Victimization Survey data shows that "robbery and assault victims who used a gun to resist were less likely to be attacked or to suffer an injury than those who used any other methods of self-protection or those who did not resist at all." Kleck's more recent study, published in the Journal of Criminal Law and Criminology, shows that nearly half of the 2.5 million self-defense uses of firearms uses each year are reported by women. Criminologists James Wright and Peter Rossi, in a study for the U.S. Department of Justice, found that thirty-four percent of felons have been "scared off, shot at, wounded, or captured by an armed victim."

Despite Kleck's award-winning studies on the deterrent effect of firearms, many people still think that criminals are not deterred by armed citizens. Yet a study for the U.S. Department of Justice found that forty percent of felons did not commit one or more particular crimes because they feared that their potential victims were armed. In fact, after the Orlando, Florida, police organized a handgun-training program for women, an effort that was given broad coverage by the local press, the city's rape rate dropped nearly ninety percent.

According to a 1996 study by Professor John R. Lott, Jr., of the University of Chicago, "Allowing citizens to carry concealed weapons deters violent crimes," and, in fact, if "those states which did not have right-to-carry concealed gun provisions had adopted them in 1992, approximately 1,570 murders, 4,177 rapes and over 60,000 aggravated assaults would have been avoided yearly."

In addition Professor Lott discusses the issue of women having concealed-handgun permits. In his study he examines the relationship between the number of women having a right-to-carry permit and the incidence of rape. He states that "rapists are particularly susceptible to this form of deterrence. Possibly this arises since providing a woman with a gun has a much bigger effect on her ability to defend herself against a crime than providing a handgun to a man . . . the external benefits to other women from a woman carrying a concealed handgun appear to be large relative to the gain produced by an additional man carrying a concealed handgun."

It is no small wonder that by the end of 1996, thirty-one states had passed fair and equitable right-to-carry legislation for their citizens. While in the thirteen states where such legislation was enacted in 1995 and 1996 the initiative was spearheaded by women, a 1996 nationwide survey found that seventy-five percent of registered voters said they agreed that law-abiding citizens should be able to carry firearms for personal protection.

As author David Kopel explained in the July-August

1996 issue of *Policy Review*, "Whenever a state legislature first considers a concealed-carry bill, opponents typically warn of horrible consequences: Permit holders will slaughter each other in traffic disputes, while would-be Rambos shoot bystanders in incompetent attempts to thwart crime." But, Kopel notes, "it has long been clear that they (right-to-carry laws) do not threaten public safety."

In fact, to the contrary, citizens who carry firearms lawfully are far more law-abiding than the general public. The Florida Department of State reports that nearly four hundred thousand carry licenses have been issued in Florida, yet not even two-hundredths of one percent (0.02%) have been revoked because those citizens committed firearm crimes. If only the rest of the state's citizens were as law-abiding. In a letter to Governor Lawton Chiles and other state officials dated 15 March 1995, Florida Department of Law Enforcement Commissioner James T. Moore says that "from a law enforcement perspective, the licensing process has not resulted in problems in the community from people arming themselves with concealed weapons."

In Texas, less than two-hundredths of one percent (0.015%) of carry permits have been revoked. In an article by Bruce Tomaso entitled "Gun Law's Record Impresses Official," published in the *Dallas Morning News*, 11 June 1996, Texas Department of Public Safety Director Colonel James Wilson says, "It has impressed me how remarkably responsible the permit holders have been." In Virginia, less than five-hundredths of one percent (0.045%) of carry permits have been revoked. In the article "Gun Permit Law Hasn't Raised Crime" by Ted Byrd, published in *Fredericksburg Free Lance-Star,* 2 February 1996, Virginia Public Safety Secretary Jerry Kilgore says, "Virginia has not turned into Dodge City. We have not seen a problem."

According to data published by the FBI, states with right-to-carry laws have lower overall violent crime rates, compared to states without such laws. Total violent crime is eighteen percent lower, homicide is twenty-one percent lower, robbery is thirty-two percent lower, and aggravated assault is eleven percent lower. Since Florida adopted its right-to-carry law in 1987, the state's homicide, firearm homicide, and handgun homicide rates have decreased thirty-six, thirty-seven, and forty-one percent, respectively.

Those results as well as Kleck's studies clearly demonstrate that firearms give the individual, even if the victim is a female, a fighting chance. The U.S. Justice Department study showed that "victims who used guns for protection were less likely either to be attacked or injured than victims who responded in any other way."

Unfortunately, some would have us believe that owning a firearm for self-defense is a bad idea. They point to a study that stated that it is forty-three times more likely that a self-defense gun in the home will lead to death of the intended victim, a family member, or a friend rather than the death of a criminal. But that statistic only counted self-defense when a criminal or an intruder was actually killed. As the Department of Justice studies show, criminals will leave when confronted with a citizen defending his or her home with a firearm, rather than risk being injured or captured. In reality, firearms are useful for self-defense because they prevent criminals from killing, injuring, and raping their victims. Dr. Suzanna Gratia Hupp's compelling story, which you will read in the next chapter, tells the tragic story of not being allowed to have a firearm when it was needed.

Dr. Fran Haga, sociology professor at UNC/Pembroke in North Carolina, says that historically societies fail when males fail to protect the females of breeding age. She believes the current epidemic of domestic violence is proof that America is in a state of decline.

A study by the Police Foundation found that more than ninety percent of domestic murder cases occurred at residences to which police had been called previously to resolve fights. As some of the women's stories that appear in this book make clear, women in violent domestic environments should get away from those situations. The problem isn't the gun in the home, the problem is the violent person in the home. Keep the gun, and get away from the creep.

In addition, in today's America, law enforcement officers are overburdened and thinly spread. If the American woman is to feel secure walking the streets, driving her car, or living in her home, according to both Professors Lott and Kleck she must provide for her own safety.

Yet I have been asked by mothers, grandmothers, and others who enjoy the companionship of young people, how can they feel comfortable having a firearm in their home or on their person? I like to point out that according to the National Safety Council, the per capita rate of fatal firearms accidents has fallen to an all-time low. Since 1930 the U.S. population has doubled, and the number of firearms owned by the American people has quadrupled, but even so the annual number of fatal firearms accidents has come down fifty-six percent in the last sixty-five years. The key to the decrease in accidents? Education, an area in which the NRA has been the nation's undisputed leader for over 125 years.

NRA has a firearms safety program for young people. In much the same manner that we teach our children and grandchildren about stives, matches, and other hazardous material, the NRA Eddie Eagle® Gun Safety Program tells young people that if they find a gun, "Stop! Don't touch! Leave the area. Tell an adult." As a result of the sixty-four-percent reduction in firearms accidents among children, the National Safety Council and the American Legion have given the Eddie Eagle® Program their highest educational awards for its achievement in educating over eight million children in gun safety. For further information on the program, call (800) 231–0752.

It's really about personal freedom, and it's that simple. You want the freedom to move through your home, your town, your state, your country without fear of the havoc that can be wrought by criminals. You can't afford a bodyguard, the state doesn't assign each of us our own personal police officer, and your big brother faints at the sound of loud noises. Upon whom does the responsibility for assuring your freedom fall?

You. No one else. It was said, earlier. No one else on earth is as concerned about your personal safety as you are. No one is as interested in your well-being and personal safety as you are. The ultimate responsibility is yours. Like it or not, we live in an existentialistic world.

You are responsible for your own essence. For your own life. For your own safety. Anyone who tells you otherwise is wrong.

The right of self-defense is fundamental, and how you choose to exercise that right is your decision. We hope that you incorporate the common-sense ideas in this book into your daily life so that you may be safe, not sorry.

If you choose to exercise your right by purchasing a firearm, then you have the responsibility for exercising your right safely and responsibly. The premier organization that has been teaching firearm safety and responsibility for over 125 years is the National Rifle Association.

The NRA offers several introductory courses on firearm safety and shooting skills, which I consider a must for any new gun owner or anyone considering purchasing a firearm for the first time.

For example, NRA's Basic Pistol Shooting course provides ten hours of instruction and hands-on training in the safe handling of handguns, handgun parts and operation, differences between revolvers and semiautomatics, fundamentals of pistol marksmanship, shooting positions, cleaning and storage of handguns, selecting and purchasing the right handgun for you, and more. NRA has also developed a condensed, three-hour version of the Basic Pistol course called FIRST Steps, which will teach you all of the necessary firearm safety and marksmanship fundamentals. FIRST Steps can be taught in less time because you focus exclusively on your own firearm and receive one-on-one instruction from an NRA-certified instructor.

If you are considering purchasing a handgun for self-defense, NRA offers the NRA Personal Protection course. Personal Protection, with twelve hours of instruction, covers the same material as the NRA Basic Pistol Shooting course, but includes two additional lessons led by an attorney and/or law enforcement officer. These extra lessons provide you with information on the federal, state, and local laws affecting firearm ownership and use, and the laws on self-defense that apply in your particular jurisdiction.

Even if you decide that a firearm will not play a role in your personal safety strategy, I recommend that you consider learning basic firearm safety anyway. With firearms in fifty percent of U.S. households, the odds are that you will encounter a firearm at some point in your life. NRA offers a Home Firearm Safety course, which teaches only firearm safety, not marksmanship. Home Firearm Safety is a four-hour course that covers safe handling and unloading procedures for handguns, rifles, and shotguns, as well as the safe storage of firearms in the home.

NRA has over thirty-five thousand certified firearm instructors across the United States. You can call NRA's Training and Education Division at (703) 267–1430 to receive a list of NRA-certified instructors in your area.

ELEVEN

SELF-DEFENSE: THE PRACTICAL REALITY

In the pages to come you will read the very personal stories of five women: four who used firearms to defend themselves and one who could not. These are exceptional women, although no one knew it before circumstances forced them to reveal their true nature. They all learned tremendous lessons from their exposure to violence. Sammie Foust, Charmaine Klaus, Dottie Collins, Brenda Hibbitts, and Dr. Suzanna Gratia Hupp share in their own words the experiences that changed their lives. It is their hope that by understanding what happened to them, you can learn the same lessons without having to go through this kind of experience yourself.

WELL, WILL IT HELP IF I CRY?
SAMMIE FOUST

Forty-nine-year-old Sammie Foust, five foot eight and slender, arrived in South Florida by way of Old Miss, the University of Alabama, and Chattanooga, Tennessee. She talks so slowly that any comedian in Vegas can tell three jokes in her pauses between words. But don't think she's some soft Southern belle. A housebreaker made that mistake. It was his last one.

"I had the misfortune of having a stroke at the age of thirty-five," said Sammie. "Three weeks prior I'd had a full battery of tests run at the University of Alabama at Birmingham, regular checkup type thing, and they said I was healthy as a horse, go back to the barn and have some oats. The next thing I know I had a stroke.

"The doctors, in all their infinite wisdom, determined that I had an 'arterial vascular accident,' which in stroke language is the same as someone saying you have a virus when your tummy hurts. In other words, we don't know what the hell it is but whatever it is, you got it.

"Although my family and I lived in Cleveland, Tennessee, at the time, I was taken to a hospital in Chattanooga. The doctor who worked on me, a neurologist, had all the personality and bedside manners of a rusty doorknob. I had difficulty speaking and when I could speak the wrong words came out.

If I meant to say balloon, I'd say umbrella or something equally far removed. But I tried to keep a sense of humor about it. After all, there wasn't anything I could do about it. So I figured, let's just work through it and get on about business. So I always joked about things, trying to be as positive as I could be.

"I should mention that I was in intensive care at this time and most people in intensive care don't joke too much. Finally, this doctor came in with his excuse for a personality and said, 'Don't you realize you're dying?'

"Since I couldn't speak as rapidly as he could I reached up and grabbed a pen out of his shirt pocket and wrote on the bed sheet, 'Well, will it help if I cry?'

"You have to understand that this doctor took himself very seriously, and when he was around, the nurses always backed away from him. He had his whole entourage with him, but when they saw what I'd written they all started laughing and snickering.

"He read what I wrote and said, 'No!' Then he snatched his pen out of my hand and rushed out of the room.

"As soon as he was gone, they broke up laughing. Then they stripped the sheet off the bed and hung it up on the wall behind the nurses' station.

"Anyway, that's kinda been my philosophy for a long time and that's the way I feel about this thing. Some folks may think I'm whistling past the graveyard, but for the life of me I can't see how it'll help one single solitary thing if I cry."

"This thing" Sammie speaks of took place during the early morning hours of Friday, May 10, 1996. She had been up all night working in the house, baked a couple of casseroles for the freezer, straightened some things in the master bedroom. She was expecting a visit from her son and his wife so she was getting things in order. Noticing that it was becoming daylight, she opened the sliding glass door to let the cat in, and left it ajar about four inches. She went back to the bedroom and turned on the TV to the news to get the time. It was exactly 6:23 A.M.

"I leaned back on the bed to change the channel and heard the blinds on the window rattle, and I just assumed it was the cat going out. I don't know if I shut my eyes and dozed off, but a couple of moments later I turned toward the doorway and saw a male figure barreling through. He was wearing a stocking mask, dark clothes, and while all the newspaper articles said he was wearing gloves he actually had socks on his hands. By the time I knew what was going on, he had one hand over my mouth and the other one holding one of those box-cutter razor blades at my neck."

The attacker was James Wayne Horne, thirty-six-year-old convicted burglar. He wanted Sammie's money. She pointed to her purse, then reached for it, and handed it to him. Horne dumped the contents of the purse and pawed through them, then waved the razor in her face, saying, "I want your big money."

Sammie directed him to a jewelry box on a nearby table and he dumped it, examined it, pronounced it "shit," then hit her with a closed fist. Her nose was broken and her left eye was ruptured. Because she was hit several times, the order in which the injuries occurred is a blur to her. She pointed to some other jewelry further down on the table, and when he moved Sammie reached for her gun.

"The whole thing is very strange," said Sammie. "At first it was funny to me that someone would break in at daylight. You'd think they'd do it at night when everyone's asleep, or in the daytime when no one's home. But I'd been so active in the house he might have thought, 'Well, she's finally gone to bed,' and went for it. The cops said he was loaded to the gills on all kinds of drugs, so maybe that explains it.

"The fact that I had a loaded gun at hand is more than bizarre. I'd spent the two days before the burglary cleaning out drawers and I had stuff spread all over the place. When I opened one drawer, I found two guns, a .25 and a .32. I knew I owned them, but I didn't remember where I had placed them. Lying next to the little one were four bullets, so I thought, 'Well, I ought to see if I can load it just in case I ever need it,' and I put the bullets in the magazine. I wasn't even sure I was putting the right bullets in the right magazine because they were real hard to make fit, so I put the magazine in the gun and pulled back the slide and everything worked. Then I put the safety on and set the gun on the stand by the bed. Never thought any more about it. I live alone, my kids are grown and away from home. I don't have to worry about little kids getting their hands on a gun and accidentally shooting themselves.

"And at that, I don't even know why I thought to do it, because the last time I fired a gun was when I was about fourteen years old, and that was either a rifle or a shotgun. I'd never fired a pistol in my life. I don't know why he didn't see it, as it was in plain sight.

"Another thing is that while the whole thing just took a short while, it's like everything happened in slow motion. I can see and remember every detail, they're videotaped in my mind. I can see it all frame by frame, because that's the way it happened, in slow motion, frame by frame.

"All I could think to do was to shoot at the biggest part of his body, which was his belly, so when he turned, that's what I did. At the time I thought I missed, but the autopsy showed I hit him in the mouth. He turned and lunged toward me and I shot again, still aiming for the belly. That one got him in the chest and the coroner said it was the one that ultimately killed him. At the time it didn't even slow him down.

"He slugged me again and grabbed hold of me. All I could think about was, 'Dear God, don't let me pass out,' and, 'Don't let go of that gun.' I have never gripped anything so tightly in my life. As strong as he was, he couldn't get the gun out of my hand. We were fighting breast to breast, so the gun was between us. Even though this was happening rapidly I remember thinking, 'Don't be an idiot and end up shooting yourself.' So I turned my head slightly to the side and fired the gun up from just below his chest. After three tries I finally hit him in the belly.

"He continued to fight, if anything he fought harder, and that's when we fell back through the dining room doorway to the master bedroom. We were still breast to breast. He was slamming me into walls and tables, beating me in the head, doing pretty much what he wanted except getting the gun away, and I managed to get off one more shot. That one was at a down angle and ended up in his groin.

"With the last blow he landed to my head, I fell back toward the bedroom doorway. He still had hold of my wrist, trying to get the gun, and as I fell he fell on top of me. He weighed almost two hundred pounds and I was pinned down. There was just nowhere to go and I thought it was over for me. He's choking me, I can feel I'm about to lose it, I don't know what to do, and I think I'm going to die. I'm not very religious, but in my mind I started to pray. I asked God to forgive me; I even asked him to forgive the son of a bitch who was killing me, and I prepared to die. At that very moment, he puked blood all over me and died."

Sammie was in such pain and so covered in blood, she had no idea if she was badly hurt or not. What was worse, she was pinned to the floor by the corpse of a very large man on top of her. Finally she worked her way out from under him and ran to a neighbors' house. They refused to answer the door. A very old woman who lived in the next house answered Sammie's repeated pleas to call the police by telling her she couldn't "bleed on my grass" and to "go on home."

She headed to another house, one where some friends resided, but they weren't home, so she ended up walking down the middle of the street, broken nose, ruptured eye, black and blue, covered in blood, until someone finally agreed to call the police.

"There was obviously a patrol car in the area because it took less than two minutes to show up. However, he would not come anywhere near the house. He stopped about half a block up, got out of his car, and waited for backup. Within a matter of moments there were six or seven patrol cars surrounding the area. Cape Coral police are extremely responsive and professional. They've been tremendously supportive of me all through this.

"On the scene there was a Fire Department EMS group as well as an ambulance. I was so rattled, I kept refusing to get into the ambulance, just kept saying, 'I want to go home, y'all drag him out and just let me go back home, I'll be all right.' I wanted so badly to just lock myself up in my house. I felt I'd fought for it, almost died for it, someone else did die for it, and by God, that house is mine.

"Of course, I had no idea how badly I was hurt. When I finally looked at myself in a mirror I understood why people didn't want to open the door for me, a crazy woman in a duster, beat to hell and covered in blood, not that that excuses them. One officer pulled up into the driveway, and I guess he was more or less assigned to look after me. I was just pacing around there, standing around looking while the police did their thing. Finally he talked me into sitting down in his car, so I plopped down in the backseat with my legs hanging out the door.

"When he turned to walk away I realized I had my hand in the pocket of the robe I was wearing, and the gun was still clenched in my hand. I said to him, 'Would you like to have this gun?' He turned around and said, 'Oh shit, she's still got the weapon!'

"He went across the street and got a plastic bag and the two of us worked to get the gun out of my hand. I'd gripped it so hard my hand was frozen around it. I actually thought we were going to have to break my fingers to pry it loose.

"Finally I got into the ambulance, and the people were telling me, 'You did good,' over and over again. This is while the cops were looking around and doing their thing. There were police and emergency people all over the place, but there was still no report on what they found in the house. They were being very careful, surrounding the house, checking this and that with their guns drawn. I kept saying, 'I don't know what they're worried about, I killed him.' Someone said, 'We'll know in a minute.'

"It turns out it was the first time in Lee County and the surrounding area that there was a case where the victim survived and the criminal did not. I later learned there were only thirty-six such cases in the United States in the past year.

"It was a hellova price to pay. My nose was broken, my lips were busted, two teeth were knocked out, the cap off another one was knocked off, all my teeth were loosened and the result is gum damage that still isn't resolved. The left eye was ruptured and full sight has not and will not be recovered in that eye. I still have trouble with my throat from being strangled."

Sammie asked that I include her heartfelt compliments to the Cape Coral Police Department, which she acknowledges was tremendously sensitive to her needs. She is also thankful for the state of Florida victim's advocate system, which not only paid her medical bills but supplied ongoing assistance. Not many states have such a system and as Sammie put it, "I didn't know such a thing existed before this happened. It's great to see tax money go for something that actually works for a change. A tragedy like this can break you both financially and emotionally."

Sammie's story also has the element of betrayal. Some years earlier, her youngest daughter had befriended a young girl with severe personal and family problems and asked Sammie to help. She did; in fact the girl lived with them for a while. Time passed, the girl moved on, and they had sparse contact with her except for periodic phone conversations. From time to time the girl would do housework for Sammie.

Four weeks before the shooting Sammie called her, getting in touch through her mother. She called the new number and a guy answered the phone; he told Sammie his name was Wayne. Two days before the incident she left word with the girl's mother that she was going to do some serious housecleaning and could use some help if the girl wanted a job. When the Victim's Advocate representative brought Sammie home from the hospital after the shooting, the girl was helping a male friend of Sammie's clean up the house.

"She was waiting for me out front when we drove up," said Sammie. "When I saw her, I sort of wondered, 'How did she find out,' but mostly I was just glad to see a friendly face. When she saw me, she just literally broke down and fell to her knees. Again, I didn't think much about it because I'd seen a mirror by then and I knew how bad I looked."

Sammie's male friend told her that the girl had called after the shooting and he'd told her to stay away but she came over anyway. He said she kept asking who called her girlfriend's house at ten-thirty in the morning from Sammie's house. Her girlfriend wasn't home but she had Caller ID and the machine logged the call.

"That didn't make any sense," continued

Sammie, "because at ten-thirty in the morning we were all at the hospital and the only people in the house were cops. The only reason the cops called that number is because the car that was left all night in the vacant lot next door was registered to the girl's friend. It was the car Horne drove to the area."

It turned out that Horne had lived with the girl's friend but moved out. He then stayed with the young girl and her husband for a couple of weeks. He left, they maintained, two weeks before the incident. The young girl admitted that Sammie had been a topic of discussion. She had mentioned that Sammie lived in a nice house on the good side of town and had always been a good friend and generous to her. But when Sammie spoke to her four weeks prior to the incident, she'd told the girl a story that could have made her think there was "big money" in the house. It was a personal story told casually and offhand in the way people do when they're talking with someone they trust. Horne learned of Sammie Foust through someone she had befriended and helped.

"I've lived alone since my daughter moved out in 1992," said Sammie. "I've never been what you'd call a 'scaredy-cat,' but my friends and family constantly told me that I should have a gun. I always told them I didn't need one, but I finally accepted this .25-caliber gun as a gift from a friend.

"My father, who is a big hunter, loves dogs and guns, was also on me to get one, so when I got the .25 I called him and told him I had it. He just raised all kinds of hell, flat threw a fit, not because I got a gun but because I got a small one.

"He said, 'Do you not remember, all your life I've told you that a wounded mad dog is dangerous and dead dogs don't bite!'

"That phrase ran through my mind when I picked up the gun and pointed it, and comes back to me over and over again. If you're going to shoot, shoot to kill, because a wounded mad dog is even madder and dead dogs don't bite.

"I am very, very regretful that someone had to die, but I'm equally glad it wasn't me. That was the choice I had to make. I made it and I chose to live."

OUR RIGHT TO SELF-DEFENSE
CHARMAINE KLAUS

Charmaine Klaus lives in an unincorporated township in Oakland County, Michigan, two miles from the city of Pontiac. It's an interesting area, socially and demographically. Every ethnic group in America is found there, and with the exception of the city of Pontiac, the county has a lower crime rate than Canada.

Pontiac is considered a high crime area, even though, demographically, it's not a whole lot different than the rest of the county. Perhaps the reason is that Pontiac has a police chief who openly brags he hasn't issued a single concealed-carry permit in the city. Law-abiding citizens in the rest of Oakland can get a permit to carry firearms if they meet the state-set criteria. The conclusion is obvious.

Charmaine managed a "Stop N Rob" (convenience store) two blocks away from her home for some time, but was transferred to another one in Clarkston, another little bedroom community near Pine Bluff. It was another low crime area, but there was a batch of convenience store robberies in the sparsely populated outlying areas. The stores getting hit were manned by only one clerk. The thieves would rob the stores, then take the clerks out in the woods, where they tortured and killed them.

The store's supervisor had told the managers and clerks not to carry guns. If a robbery was attempted, they were to give up the money. If they wanted to take you out of the store, simply refuse to go.

"I see," I said, when Charmaine told me the above. "No, Mr. Robber, I'm not going. Something like that?"

"Exactly," she said. "If the guy is going to kill you, make him do it in the store."

She told her husband about the new rules and he got angry. Neither of them liked the odds of getting caught unarmed by a crew like that. After some discussion between then, they decided she would carry and simply not tell anyone about it.

One Saturday night, a nineteen-year-old girl, Darlene Ramsey, was working at Charmaine's store. It was to be her last weekend on the job. She was to start work as a medical technician the next week. It was about ten-thirty at night, that was when Charmaine counted out the shift, leaving the clerk only twenty dollars in change to work with during the process. Charmaine was in a small, eight-by-eight back room that served as an office, counting money.

"All of a sudden Darlene came running in the door, saying there was a masked man with a gun coming in the store," said Charmaine. "I said, 'Lock the door and call the police.' I started to dial as she started to lock up, and the guy shot right through the door. She went back against the door and he opened the door and shot her twice, once in the chest and once in the abdomen.

"I was on the wall where he couldn't see me and was reaching for my gun. In fact, I couldn't see him at this time. Then he came through the door and I shot him. Unfortunately the bullet hit a tooth and broke up. Even though it lodged in his throat and he was bleeding very badly, he continued the assault. I had a Smith .38 revolver; he had a Colt semiautomatic super .38.

"He just kept shooting, but he was somewhat disoriented because of the shock of being hit, and missed me. Bullets whizzed by my head and I started to crawl under the desk. He was in the hall, firing at me through the door. And then he decides to come back into the room and I'm under the desk, blocked from doing anything. He grabs Darlene and shoots her point blank in the head. Then with his last bullet he shot me.

"I could see he had the gun up by my head and at the last moment I moved my head and put up my hand. His bullet went through my hand and into my jaw. Now his gun was empty so he left, just running out of the store. I remember thinking when he came into the room that I had already hit him and he was bleeding, so even if we both died chances were they would catch him.

"Darlene was still alive when I checked her, but not for very long. The shooter had gone out the back door and the alarm went off, and the security company, instead of calling the store or the police, called my husband and told him. He told them to get the police there at once. For some reason, I couldn't use the phone in the store, it didn't work.

"I walked out into the cash register area. There were customers standing around wanting to be waited on, wanting to know what the hell was going on. I said, 'I'm sorry but we were just shot,' and a male customer panicked—started screaming and running around the store.

"Then the sheriff's department showed up and took over. Although I was pumping gallons of adrenaline, they got me settled down to some degree. An ambulance for Darlene and me arrived, and while they were loading me into it, the deputies promised me that they would look after the store, make sure it was locked up. After all that, I was still concerned with the store.

"I told them what happened and that I'd shot

the guy, so they started looking for him. For some reason they were convinced he'd go north, but instead he went south to Detroit. He went to this street where there was nothing there, and when the police came by he told them he was robbed and shot. One of the cops had heard the report of what'd happened up here and didn't buy it. They had him."

The story takes a bizarre twist at this point because the brother of the dentist who removed the bullet from the robber ended up taking it home with him. The brothers went home, and before they got there, one of them threw the bullet out. Law officers looked high and low for it and found it in a snowbank near the brothers' home.

Since the assailant was masked, Charmaine couldn't identify him. She knew the approximate height and weight, but the mask hid his facial features. He was placed at the scene by forensic analysis of his blood at the scene. They never did find the gun. Whoever got rid of it hid it very well.

Albert Joseph Hartford, Jr. and two of his nearest and dearest friends were out on bail for drug charges. They'd robbed two other convenience stores earlier in the evening, trying to raise money to pay their legal fees. Those attempts resulted in the shooting of Charmaine and the killing of Darlene Ramsey. Hartford was found guilty of first degree murder and is serving a mandatory life sentence in Michigan.

"I don't dwell on this very much anymore," said

Charmaine. "The reason why, I believe, is because I had the chance to defend myself and I did the best I could. If I hadn't had the gun, he would have killed both of us. Since then I've worked with the NRA and other organizations to try to get our right to self-defense recognized. The state police are against law-abiding citizens being able to defend themselves. We use their own statistics to show them how crime in areas where people legally carry firearms in Michigan is less than that of Canada, and they try to deny them.

"I can't imagine what it would be like to be a helpless victim in such a situation as mine. And that's what most victims of armed robberies are. First they're the victim of the criminal, then they're the victim of the system, the courts, whatever. To have to sit around and think, if only I'd done this or that, and to know that if I'd been armed I could have made things different must be unbelievably painful.

"I'm sorry Darlene was killed but I couldn't have saved her. He shot her the second he came through the door. I did the best I could and I'll spend the rest of my life working to see we don't lose our right to self-defense.

DON'T HATE
DOTTIE COLLINS

A plague has been visited on American society. It's a private plague that preys on millions of families, made even more deadly in that it does its damage behind closed doors, more insidious in that it inflicts a state of shame on its victims, and more painful in that the carriers are always loved ones. It knows no racial, social, or economic barrier, though the largest numbers of victims are women and the highest volume of carriers are men. It has rent American families asunder for generations. Though not always fatal there is no cure, no vaccine. The best one can hope for is to put it into remission or remove oneself from the proximity of the outbreak. Even then, the effects last forever, bearing weight on almost every decision victims make, coloring their relationships.

I am speaking of the plague called "domestic violence."

Spousal abuse. The physical war between men and women.

Dottie Collins lives in Oak Hills, West Virginia. She's a petite and pretty blonde of forty-five who looks a great deal younger without trying to do so. Dottie is very quiet and unassuming and in spite of her attractiveness you have to look carefully to see she's there—she has a way of making herself very small, to keep from being noticed. There's a reason, of course. Dottie Collins can tell you all you ever wanted to know about domestic violence.

Dottie met Roger at the Crossroads Lounge, a neighborhood bar in Beckley, West Virginia. A mutual friend introduced them.

"All I knew at the time was his occupation, he

was a painter and did bodywork on cars. He was divorced, forty-four years old, born and raised in the area. People knew him, grew up with him, and none gave me the least indication he had a violent nature. Whenever I'd seen him in the past he was always quiet and composed.

"I didn't ask a lot of questions. He mentioned he was divorced and had children and that he wasn't in contact with them because of a dispute over child support. That story must fit half the divorced men in America and I had no reason to think any more about it."

Roger's parents seemed like decent people. Dottie especially liked his mother. After dating for a while, she allowed Roger to move in but quickly wondered if she'd made a mistake, because Roger's temper was getting shorter and shorter, usually over nothing. A wrong word by someone, or even something he would mistake for a wrong word, would send him into a rage. He would think people were against him, think no one thought he was good enough for her, and rave about it, even though none of their friends had ever said a word against him.

"He was intensely jealous," said Dottie. "I'm a sociable person. I have a lot of what I call 'buddies,' just friends, people I talk to, maybe dance with if I see them out, that's it. Some of them I've known for years. All at once he just decided they were against him, they were trying to break us up. He didn't want me to have anything to do with anybody but him.

"He was jealous of my kids. I have a daughter who's twenty-four, she has a little boy of five—they live in Pennsylvania. I have a son who is nineteen and another one who is twenty-two. The boys were living with me at the time, although the older one has since moved to Charleston.

"I began to notice little things that didn't add up. He'd say something about his past and then his mother would say something that contradicted it. He kept getting more and more jittery, nervous, but I just let it go. I'm not one to make waves, and he hadn't hit me, yet.

"Then he did. It was during the winter, it was real cold and bitter, and we'd been more or less trapped in the trailer. My girlfriend called and wanted to come over, but I told her she couldn't because the roads were so bad down here. He just started thinking I wanted to go out, wanted to get away from him, and one word led to another. He slapped me. Immediately, he started to apologize. 'Oh baby, I'm sorry, I can't believe I did that, I've never done anything like that before, I'm so sorry,' all that kind of stuff. I let it go."

There was no more physical abuse over the next couple of months but there was a tension between them. It came to a head when Roger got into a fight with one of her children. The older one cracked wise in defense of Dottie, and Roger hit him in the face. Then the younger one, who is much larger than his brother, jumped into the scuffle and pulled Roger aside. There was only one real casualty of the spat: Dottie. She fell apart mentally and ended up in the hospital.

"Roger took me home from the hospital and we immediately got into a disagreement. This was the last thing on earth I needed. We were in my car, so I simply drove to his mom and dad's house and dropped him off, told him I was done. Stay out of my life. It worked for about a month."

Dottie ran into Roger every so often and tried to keep things friendly. Though still attracted to Roger, she was afraid of him. She and her mother went out of town for the Easter holidays and returned to find that Roger had sent a dozen roses to Dottie at her mother's house. A half an hour later he showed up at her mother's door. Dottie made the mistake of hearing him out. He apologized, swore he had his temper under control, and pledged nothing like the past would ever happen again. They started dating again.

For a short while things went okay, but then the pattern started again. The flareups, the nervousness, the accusations and jealousy, just as it was before. Not only was it back, it was progressing faster and getting worse. Dottie realized nothing was ever going to change, and started to wonder how she was going to get out of the situation.

One Friday, when she was taking him to work, they got into an argument and he hauled off and hit her with a clenched fist. This while she was driving down the road.

"On Friday nights I go out with my girlfriend," said Dottie. "When we started back dating I told him I was going to keep on doing that, and he couldn't come along because I didn't want to take a chance on him losing his temper. He agreed. This particular Friday he didn't want me to go. I told him I was going anyway.

"It's no big deal when we girls go out. I go over to her place and we get together with a couple other women to listen to music. We don't cat around. I don't even drink. I just like to dance and listen to music, enjoy talking to people. But I had no intention of giving it up or listening to someone yell at me about it. Anyway, he hit me while I was driving. Just hauled off and hit me upside the head with his fist."

She swerved to the side, righted the car, and headed on down the road, completely ignoring what had just happened. At the nearest filling station she stopped right in front of the doors, got out of the car, and told him he'd just blown his last chance. She was going inside for a minute and when she came out she wanted him gone; if he was still there when she returned she'd call the police. It worked. When she returned to her car Roger was gone. Dottie drove home.

Fifteen minutes later he was at the door. Dottie wouldn't let him in; then her son drove in behind him and Roger left quietly. Shortly afterward, he called. Dottie told him to stay away, that she didn't want to see him or talk to him, to get out of her life.

She promised if he didn't do exactly that, she'd file charges against him. He agreed.

"The rest of the day was just fine. I didn't hear from him. A friend of mine had been sick and I went over to her house that night. When I arrived all the lights were off in her house so I didn't stop, just drove a short ways past her house and turned around. As I started back in the other direction I met him coming toward me like a bat out of hell. He wheeled around and came up behind me, ramming my car twice.

"This is a mountain road and there are very few houses on it. I saw some people out in their yard so I pulled in the driveway and asked if they'd call the police. They'd heard the impact and did as I asked. Meanwhile, he'd flown on by. I used their phone to call my girlfriend and my sons back at my house to tell them what happened, and that if Roger showed his face not to let him in under any circumstances.

"The policeman checked the damage to the car and we followed him to Fayetteville. The magistrate court issued a warrant and a domestic violence order. Roger was arrested in Raleigh County and charged with reckless driving, driving without a license, driving under the influence, and fleeing from an officer.

"He got out of jail the following Tuesday. They were supposed to let me know when he was released, but through some kind of foul-up that didn't happen. Wednesday night the phone started ringing, very late. I was tired, my mother had been sick and

I'd been spending time with her, so my son answered. I didn't pay it any attention, they're young and get calls at all hours. Then it rang again. And again. And again.

"Finally, I got up to chew on my son, I wanted a little sleep that night, but he said someone was calling and hanging up whenever he answered. I asked if he'd pushed the dial-back code and he said yes, that it was a private number and the system wouldn't dial it back. It finally dawned on me what was happening, so I called the jail and they said Roger'd been released the day before.

"I called 911 and told them what was happening. They gave me a number to punch to get a trace. I couldn't get the calling number but the police could. So each time the phone rang I dialed the trace code. When the phone started again the next morning, Roger started to talk.

"I told him to leave me alone, then called the police. They sent a deputy out, who said if it happened again to go see the magistrate and file a violation of the domestic violence order. It stated that he was to have no contact with me, even through a third party. I went to the courthouse and found that the magistrate I needed to see was on vacation. The others weren't familiar with the case and suggested I wait until she got back. It seemed nothing could or would be done, so I went home."

Several days of relative quiet passed. Roger called only once and even though it was a violation of the magistrate's order, he wasn't threatening. Another Friday night rolled around. Dottie's girlfriend's brother was having a birthday party and a group planned on getting together at the bar. Dottie often stayed at her girlfriend's house when they went out and she planned to do so on this night.

On the way home from the party she remembered she'd promised her son he could have the car the next morning, and had to return home. Dottie went to her car without going into her friend's house, just waited to see that her friend got in safely. When Dottie started the car and turned around to back up she didn't see anyone, anywhere. But when she turned around to go forward, Roger was on the hood of the car with a gun in his hand. He put the gun to the windshield, yelled, "You're dead!" and pulled the trigger.

"The shot came through the windshield, caught me in the right temple, and stunned me," she said. "I fell across the passenger side. I always drive at night with my doors locked and the windows rolled up. My car is the kind that has the automatic seat belts that attach as soon as you close the door and it has the shifter between the seats. So, while the top half of me was lying across the passenger side, my lower half was still strapped into the driver's seat. I don't know how, but I didn't lose consciousness. I was stunned, but awake.

"Roger came around to the side of the car, broke in the window, and unlocked the door. He got in the car and shot me twice more. One bullet went in above the knee and came out below it. It turned out to be a fairly clean wound. My leg gives me some trouble, but the bullet didn't hit any bones or anything. The other one caught me in the left forearm, shattering the bones. Chances are I'll never regain full use of it. I've already had surgery and there is more to come to rebuild the bone."

Dottie's girlfriend heard the shots and ran outside to see what was happening. Roger fired at her and missed. She ducked behind her car. Roger turned back to Dottie, wedging his way into the car, actually sitting on the lower half of her body as he started to drive away.

The girlfriend's driveway circles around an embankment and Roger headed up it. Dottie had no idea how badly she was wounded, but assumed she would be dead in a matter of minutes. The only thing going through her mind was that she couldn't let him get away with it. She noticed she'd fallen across her pocketbook. After getting the restraining order against Roger, Dottie had bought a gun from a friend, a little .25 automatic. It was in her pocketbook.

Without him knowing it, Dottie managed to get the gun in her hand. Roger probably thought she was dead. Although she had hold of the gun, she couldn't aim it. She simply pointed it in Roger's general direction and emptied the magazine.

"I had no idea if I hit him or not. I couldn't see

anything at the time, but I could feel the car go over the embankment and drop about thirty feet. The last clear thought in my mind was when Roger got out of the car. He screamed at the top of his lungs, 'I hope you're dead, I hope I've killed you!' From then on it's a blank until I woke up in the hospital.

"They later informed me I'd got out of the car, walked through the brush, across a creek, up the hill to my girlfriend's house, and come straight in her front door. She was on the phone at the time talking to the police. They said I walked into the kitchen, sat down at the table, took off my earrings, and told her to call an ambulance. I don't remember a thing about it.

"I didn't know I'd hit Roger, didn't know where he went, didn't know anything until two days later when I woke up in the hospital. They told me I'd hit him twice, he'd been arrested and was in jail. While I was in the hospital they kept me under very tight security. I was not even listed under a name, I was listed under a number. My own mother had problems getting in to see me. They had Roger's picture posted throughout the hospital."

The police arrested Roger when he went for medical treatment. One of Dottie's shots hit him in the hand, another lodged in his jaw. Roger has pleaded not guilty and since there are multiple jurisdictions involved, while he's in jail in Raleigh County under a $50,000 bond he can't be released until he clears with Fayette County. The police found out later that he'd broken into the girlfriend's trailer earlier that night and waited inside for them to come home. If Dottie'd walked in the house with her girlfriend, chances are he would have killed both of them.

"I didn't have a license to carry at that point. I do now. I've taken the NRA's handgun training course and just received my concealed-carry license.

"I bought the gun, a small .25-caliber semiautomatic, after he ran me off the road. The day after I bought it, I had my son buy a box of shells and load it, then never gave it another thought until I needed it. I never shot the gun, in fact I'd never shot a pistol before. I know people raise hell about small guns, 'Saturday Night Specials' or some such. All I can say is on a particular Friday night a 'Saturday Night Special' saved my life."

For a woman like Dottie to have come to the point in her life where she was capable of defending herself in the manner that she did is just as miraculous as the fact that she is alive today.

Dottie was born and raised in a "hollow" in central West Virginia called Long Shoal Run. A hollow is a place between two hills, a small valley with a creek, perhaps, and some level land here and there for houses. It was a place of hardy and self-sufficient people. Most of the men were coal miners, and everyone farmed a little, even if it was only a garden with vegetables for personal use. The farming was done by horse and by hand.

The coal mines weren't large corporate concerns,

they were small, independent mines. Many times she saw her grandfather and her uncles come home with bleeding backs because the spaces they mined were so small they had to crawl in on their backs and dig out the coal with short-handle picks. Coal was not pulled out with mechanical equipment but by ponies pulling carts.

It was a hard life and created hard people. Physical and mental abuse by parents and spouses was the way of life. It was accepted by the women.

"Practically all the men where I grew up would go out on the weekends, get drunk, lay up with whatever trollop was passing through, then go home and beat the hell out of their wives. It was the rule, not the exception, and I never knew of a wife who ever left because of it. It's just the way things were."

Although Dottie was raised by strict grandparents, whom she loved dearly, she dropped out of school at thirteen and at nineteen she married a guy from the next hollow, the brother of their nearest neighbor.

Her husband was twelve years older than she and in some ways treated her more like a child than a spouse. He had many friends but would allow her to have none, went out when he felt like it but kept her close to home. He did all the shopping for the family, even to the extent of buying her maternity clothes.

He also subjected her to constant mental abuse. She was told she was stupid, homely, couldn't do anything right, and it was continual. The marriage continued for seventeen years. In that time she literally does not recall her ex-husband saying a single nice thing. When he wasn't abusive, he was silent, always controlling. During the last ten years of the marriage she started preparing herself to leave. She learned to drive, worked on developing an attitude of independence among the kids, and even got a job. She worked days as a hostess in a Chinese restaurant, at night she washed dishes. Those are the kinds of jobs available to junior high dropouts.

Finally, taking her daughter with her Dottie fled from her abusive husband to the neighboring state of Maryland. Unfortunately she drifted into another relationship that was even more abusive than her marriage, one that almost saw her killed. She never filed charges on the individual because he had friends in the police force of the small Maryland town and she feared nothing would be done. Finally she managed to get away from him. Then her mother became ill and Dottie moved back to West Virginia.

By this time she'd soaked up enough abuse from enough men who said they loved her to qualify for disability. She knew she had a problem that was more than just bad luck in picking men, so she started therapy. In doing so she was surprised to find that spousal abuse is not limited to hollows in West Virginia or waitresses in Maryland, that it happens on Park Avenue, in Beverly Hills, and everywhere in between. When she met Roger, the man who ultimately shot her, she was aware of the pattern of her life and was trying to do something about it.

He fooled her originally, but rather than continue to put up with the abuse, she had become strong enough to try to get him out of her life. Getting shot was the result of that effort.

She was truly surprised to learn there are people like Detective J. E. Bare from the Raleigh County West Virginia Sheriff's Department, who supported her after Roger attacked her. But she still gets angry at people, especially women, who haven't had the experiences and make value judgments about those who have.

"The first thing they say is, 'I don't know why you put up with that, I'd never let a man do that to me.' Maybe they're telling the truth or maybe they just think they are, I don't know. I do know that when you've got kids, no education, no money, and no place to go, you'll put up with a lot of things to keep clothes on your kids' backs and food on the table for them. Add to that the fact you're consistently told you're useless, worth nothing, that everyone thinks you're as dumb and ugly as homemade soap, and you come to believe this is all you have coming in life. Now I know it's not true, but I had to be beat almost to death to learn that lesson.

"I hope someone, somewhere, reads this, and instead of feeling completely ignorant and isolated like I did, will look around and find the help that is available. It's there. Yes, you have to look for it, but it's there.

"I hope they don't waste time being afraid of the

police like I did. I just assumed I was as worthless as the men in my life told me I was, and that the police only existed to help the upper crust. It's not true. Maybe it was true in the past but it's not now. The Raleigh and Fayette County sheriff's departments have been tremendous. Especially Detective Bare. I don't know if they have a school for handling domestic abuse victims or what, but he's been great. He paid attention to what I told him, answered all my questions, and treated me like I was a human being, not some statistic on a piece of paper.

"So if this is happening to someone who's reading this, get help. If there is help for me, there is help for you.

"When you get help and start on the road to your new life, leave all of the old life behind you. Don't drag your pain along. And most important of all, don't hate. If you hate the person who abused you, that person still controls a piece of your soul. When you hate you're not on the road to your new life, you're still the victim of your abuser. The abuse has just taken a new form.

"Don't hate."

JUST RIGHT
BRENDA HIBBITTS

Brenda Hibbitts, an attractive forty-year-old woman with reddish brown hair and green eyes, is as gracious and as friendly as can be. You can see her good nature in her eyes, which glisten brightly when she smiles, mist up with affection and pride when she tells stories about her loved ones, and laugh happily when she tells a joke. But I wouldn't care to see those eyes the way a wannabe burglar saw them last spring. I suspect they were iced over and spouting green fire at the same time. At any rate, the intruder got more than he bargained for.

"It was a Sunday," began Brenda. "I'd been working Saturdays, which makes for a long week, and I was taking a day to myself. My husband and son had just left for church and I was alone, doing some laundry, just sitting around in a gown and a housecoat. There is a community cemetery just down the road and we'd seen some folks parked there that morning. We didn't pay it much attention because it's not that unusual to see a car there. Anyway, the phone rang, it was a friend of mine. I also do hair and she wanted me to fix hers; we were just talking about this and that, nothing earthshaking, when there was a crash at the front door. It was so loud she heard it on the phone, even asked, 'What in the world was that?'

"'I don't know,' I said. I had a big thick wooden door. Then I heard glass breaking—there was a glass inset in the door. I had my purse sitting by the couch where I was sitting and I just grabbed my gun out of it (a 9mm Lady Smith).

"I stood up and looked down the hall and there were three people standing there. One was a great big ol' guy, about six one or six two and two-forty, muscular, looked like a boxer. He was in front and holding a hammer. Two smaller people were behind him. I thought they were both men at the time, that one of them was real young, but it turned out to be a girl. They just stood there for a second and looked at me.

"I said, 'What are you doing in my house?' I mean, it's such a surprise, they were in on me just like that. I've still got the phone at my ear, gun in the other hand. My friend says, 'What's going on?' I said, 'My God, they're in on me. Call 911.' And then I hung up the phone. Portable phone, I flicked it off, I'm just standing there with the phone in one hand and the gun in the other.

"I looked at them and I said, 'Get out of my house or I'll kill you.'

"He just looked at me, that was when I noticed he had a hammer in his hand. He raised the hammer and I took a step back. Then he took a step forward and I fired a shot. It was the first time I ever fired that gun. I thought I'd missed him because he had no change in expression at all. The three of them ran into the bedroom next to the hall.

"I yelled at them, 'Get out of there, if I have to come in there I'm going to kill every one of you.' Of course, I wasn't about to go in there because I thought there was a gun in that room. The day before, my son had had his rifle in the closet, a .22 with a thirty-round clip. I'd told him to put it up, but sometimes telling kids to do something don't have all the effect it ought to. It turned out he'd put the gun where it belonged, but I didn't know that at the time.

"There are two doors to that room and I put myself in position where I could see both of them and still have some cover if they came out shooting. So I tried again to bluff them out. I yelled again, 'If I have to come in there I'll kill every one of you.'

About the time I yelled, the guy I shot jumped out into the hall. When he did I put the gun right between his eyes and he started begging me not to shoot him again. He said, 'I'll leave if you just won't shoot me again.'

"I said, 'It's your choice how you leave but you're going, one way or the other.'

"While he was begging, the others ran out the second door. That suited me fine, I knew they weren't that much of a threat. When I shot him I had time to shoot one of the other two, but I didn't. The one I had a clear shot at looked like a thirteen-year-old boy and I didn't want to shoot a kid if I didn't absolutely have to. I have a thirteen-year-old boy. Come to find out that was a girl. She wasn't a child, she's about twenty-five years old, but she's small and wore a baseball cap. I just thought it was a kid.

"Anyway, I let him go. I didn't know it, but there were two more of them in a van down the hill. My husband had seen the van, it was a blue thing with five bullet holes in the windshield and no, I didn't put them there. I shot only once and that one hit the man I shot at right in the chest with a hollow-point.

"Somehow, he made it back to the van, it was about a hundred and fifty yards away, and they took off. I never saw the van, that's what the cops told me. Anyway, they went to the hospital and threw the wounded man out on a picnic table and took off. A nurse saw them do it and described the same van my husband saw here at the house.

"The police found the van and found two of the others in it. Somewhere or another they got the rest of them. I don't know too much more about it. One of the girls made bail, the rest of them, three males and a female, are still in custody and awaiting trial. Three of them were from Crossville, Tennessee, which is west of Knoxville, about a hundred and fifty miles from here. The guy I shot is from Florida and the girl in the baseball cap lived around here for a while. I'm told they're all wanted in Tennessee, that there was stuff in the van from other robberies in other places. How in the world they all got together, found their way out here in the hills, and decided to rob this house is a mystery to me. I do know that they saw my husband leave out of here and they knew I was in here alone and I do know, in my own mind, that they were going to kill me.

"I don't know why. I work in a pawn shop, maybe they thought they could take me up there and make me open it up, I just don't know. You can live in Laurel County all your life and know the area, then let me give you directions how to get to my house and you're still going to have a hard time finding it. You don't just wake up one morning and drive up here from Crossville, Tennessee, and decide to rob this place.

"My husband knew something was going to happen. I don't mean on that particular day, but he'd been edgy, like he was expecting trouble. I spend a lot of time by myself, and I don't know how many times in the weeks before it happened he'd asked if I had my gun and was it loaded.

"People are always asking if I'm handling it, how am I doing and all that, isn't it just terrible you had to shoot somebody. As if I'm supposed to be sorry I did it. Well, it is terrible to have to shoot somebody the way I did. You're in your home, you're supposed to be safe. I didn't ask them to come here and I didn't want to hurt anyone. But shooting the fellow I shot means no more to me than shooting a sick dog. In fact, it don't even bother me. What bothers me is that I might have to look over my shoulder for the rest of my life if they have friends or family who want to get even.

"I've had a tremendous amount of support for what I did. People are always telling me how proud they are of me and things like that. One of the law officers told me I wouldn't believe how many trained police officers wouldn't be able to do what I did. He said people get excited and miss, or they freeze, or any number of things happen.

"Some others, including my husband, have said maybe I should have killed the whole bunch of them. I don't think so. Maybe there is a reason why I didn't, maybe one or more of those folks will get a chance to learn their lesson and be a decent person after this. All I know is, someone tried to break into my house and I stopped them. That's what I feel I was supposed to do and I believe I did just right.

"That gun saved me and that's all there is to that. If, instead of raising so much cain about guns, people would teach their kids what they're for and how to use them, we wouldn't have all this kind of mess we have with kids killing each other and all that.

"I was raised around guns. I don't shoot like my husband and son do, but I know what I'm doing with a gun. Since this happened I've started practicing with a pistol and learning how to shoot a rifle and a shotgun. I'll always have a gun and I'll always keep this one," she said, showing off her Lady Smith. "In fact, I just might have it bronzed."

WHAT IT ALL COMES DOWN TO
Dr. Suzanna Gratia Hupp

A quick glance at Suzy Gratia can be deceiving. She's extremely attractive, with slim features, high cheekbones and forehead, shining bright blue eyes, and a smile that's never more than a heartbeat away. She doesn't look like someone with great strength or resolve until she starts talking about gun laws and what should be the right of all Americans—the right to carry a concealed weapon.

Then her demeanor changes. She stands straighter, the softness leaves her eyes—they flash anger and dedication. Suddenly you realize you're standing in the presence of a serious player in today's world; you're standing in the presence of pure conviction and strength.

Dr. Suzanna Gratia Hupp, a thirty-six-year-old chiropractor from Lampasas, Texas, who never figured to be on the front page of *USA Today*, understands the need to defend oneself better than most. As they say in Texas, she's "been there, done that, and didn't like it very much." She survived the massacre at Luby's Cafeteria in Killeen, Texas, on October 16, 1991. Her mother and father did not.

All they wanted was to have a quiet lunch at Luby's. It didn't seem too much to ask of a beautiful October day. Suzy didn't particularly want to go. Her friend Mark Kopenhafer was the manager on duty at the cafeteria. He'd called earlier and asked her to drop by for lunch, but she declined, too much to do. Then, just before noon, her parents dropped by the clinic and asked her to join them.

Al and Ursula Gratia were fun people and their three children treasured the time they spent with them. Al had retired from the heavy equipment business a little over three years before and they'd moved to the hill country of Texas to be near their children. Suzy had a chiropractic clinic in Copperas Cove, son Allan had one in Lampasas, and daughter Erika was an area schoolteacher.

Ursula's life was her family. They'd get together without notice for lunch or dinner or games or just to have a drink and watch the sunset. Al spent the first two hours of every day at the municipal golf course and the rest of the day at the computer or in the library. He was writing a book. Two weeks before, the couple had celebrated their forty-seventh anniversary. So when Suzy's parents dropped by the clinic and asked her to go to lunch at Luby's, she went. Time spent with them was always a pleasure.

Luby's was packed on October 16, 1991. It was a Wednesday—"Take Your Boss to Lunch Day," and the day after payday—so the Gratia family couldn't get their usual table, which turned out to be a blessing. While they were sipping their after-lunch coffee and chatting, the world ended. George Hennard, thirty-five, of Belton, Texas, crashed his pickup truck through the window of the restaurant, running over their usual table, and calmly started shooting people.

"We were at the 'piddling' stage," said Suzy. "We'd finished eating and were waiting for Mark to come back from checking on something, when this guy drives through the window. I mean, the entire truck came through, and then he hit his brakes and slammed it into park, so the vehicle just sat there and bounced up and down. He plowed through a few tables and whatnot, and of course, I thought it was an accident. I started to get up to help because he'd injured a number of people when he plowed in. Mark was on his way back to the table, and he grabbed one of the ladies with the serving carts and pulled her back out of the way. About the time I got halfway up we heard the first gunshots.

"I didn't see him raise the gun and fire but Mark did. As soon as we heard the shots we dropped to the floor, turned over a table, and got behind it. We're thinking it's a robbery, but the shooting continues. And he was not spraying bullets, there'd be a pop, a second later another one, then another one. He was taking aim, big time.

"Mark told me later Hennard took his first couple of shots before he ever got out of the truck, fired a couple shots at the serving line, then he got out of the truck. From that point on he was just executing people.

"You expect an explanation, you know, like in the movies. Someone says, 'This is a stickup, get out your wallets!' but there was no explanation, he just kept shooting people. Then I start to think—again, too much TV—I start to think, 'It's a hit.' It's 'Boss's Day,' maybe there is someone important here and this guy's going to kill him, but the shooting continues.

"I keep waiting for someone to do something

because there are always DPS (Texas Department of Public Safety) officers or cops in there, but we found out later he'd sat out in the parking lot and waited for some police officers to leave. It took a good forty-five seconds to figure out what was going on. He killed six or seven people before I decided, this guy is just going to walk around and shoot people. That is not the first thing that comes to mind.

"At that point he walks around the front of his truck and is about fifteen feet from me, and I thought, 'I got this turkey.' I remember this so vividly, 'I got this turkey.' He had his back three-quarters turned to me, he was shooting with his right hand, and I had him. I guess I could have missed but that's not real likely. Everyone in the place was down, he was standing straight, the table was up, I had a place to prop my arm, he was mine.

"But there was nothing I could do. If only I could have carried my gun in my purse, then I might have had a chance. Instead, my gun, a .38-caliber Smith and Wesson Airweight, was in my car, a hundred yards away on the other side of the building. I thought, 'What do I do now, throw my purse at him?'

"We had no way out. We were up in a corner, there was a wall maybe twelve feet away, and he was blocking the nearest exit. The only other exit was way on the other side. I remember looking at a sugar shaker, at a butter knife, anything to use against him. There was nothing.

"The guy had complete control of the situation, it wasn't a melee, it was quiet, which you wouldn't expect. You'd occasionally hear someone say, 'Oh, my God,' or a scream, but mostly it was just quiet. Even the gunshots were quiet, they were just pops, which I guess is a testimony to the wonderful acoustics of the place, or something.

"About then my father raised up into a crouched position and said, 'I've got to do something, I've got to do something, he's going to kill everybody in here.' Later on I read about an elderly couple killed and I didn't relate them to my parents. Dad, seventy-one, but he was a long way from being some kind of doddering old man.

"I grabbed him and tried to pull him down, but when Dad saw his chance he broke free and went at the guy. But, like I said, Hennard had total control. You could not rush him. It might have worked if you could somehow coordinate with ten other guys to rush him at once and then he only takes five of you out.

"Dad covered maybe half the fifteen or twenty feet to the guy when he turned and shot him in the chest. Dad fell facing me. He was still alive and semi-conscious but when I saw the wound I more or less wrote him off. There was no way he could live with that kind of hole in him.

"Then something caught the guy's attention and he moved off in another direction. I got my first good look at his face and I just couldn't understand the deal. I thought, 'What is this guy's problem, he's good-looking, well built, he's got a new truck, I'd probably go out with him. What can be so wrong in his life that he'd do something like this?' But I never saw his eyes, and those who did said he was just totally insane. The lights were on but nobody was home. Anyway, he walked to the wall and had a choice of coming either toward me or away from me. As fate would have it, he walked away from me.

"A customer or kitchen worker at the back of the restaurant broke out a window, and I'm thinking, 'Oh Lord, there are more of them.' I'm still looking for an explanation, thinking terrorists or some such thing. Then I saw people going out the window. It was a long way away, but I registered it in my mind as a potential means of escape. When the guy had his back to me I reached around and grabbed my mom and said, 'Come on, come on. We gotta get outta here.' I pulled her up and she didn't say anything. Again I said, 'Come on, we gotta go," and we headed for the window. At least I thought we did.

"The second I got out the window Mark came out a side door and said, "Where's your parents?"

"Dad's inside, shot," I said, then turned to help Mom out the window, but she wasn't there.

"We learned later that she'd moved to Dad and cradled his head in her lap. The gunman walked over to her, she looked up at him, then lowered her head. He killed her on the spot."

Suzy paused to catch her breath. She's told this story so many times she knows exactly what people want to hear and it all sort of comes out at once. We're sitting around the kitchen table in her home in the hills above Lampasas. Since the Killeen incident she married Greg Hupp, a tall, slender Ph.D. candidate in health psychology who is almost as reserved as Suzy is vibrant. She's seven-and-a-half-months pregnant.

I keep looking at her for cracks in her facade, thinking to myself that no one is this together, but the cracks aren't there. There is no facade. Suzy is Suzy; what you see and hear is what you get.

"What do you feel about Hennard?" I asked.

"Nothing," she said, and noting my surprise, continued.

"Look, you don't hate a rabid dog. The dog can't help that it's rabid. You simply do what has to be done, which is take it behind the barn and shoot it. You don't go overboard one way or the other, hating it, feeling compassion for it, you just put it out of its misery as soon as you can so it doesn't hurt anyone else. If it had been a career criminal, that would have been one thing, but this was a guy who woke up with worms for brains.

"That doesn't mean I don't have a lot of anger over the situation. I've become an activist because I'm angry, I do all the media work I do because I'm angry, and I'm running for the legislature because I'm angry.

"I'm angry at the legislators and the laws that robbed me of the basic human right to defend my parents and myself from a murderous attack, and I'm angry at myself for obeying such a damn stupid law in the first place.

"A woman in the area told me, not too long ago, how glad she is that I'm campaigning for concealed-carry and other gun rights. Her daughter was in Luby's that day, and she also had her gun in her car. Her daughter wasn't as lucky as I was. Her daughter was murdered.

"The other thing is that the media has all these professional victims they trot out every time something happens, and they always go on the tube telling their 'poor me' stories. The first thing they do is start hollering for more gun control or outright bans. I thought it was time there was a woman around who spoke realistically from a different point of view.

"It wasn't a gun that killed people in Luby's. It was the nut holding the gun who did the killing. He could have run his truck around inside and over people and killed just as many or thrown in a bottle of gasoline or done any number of things. No one would be hollering to do away with pickup trucks or gasoline, but as soon as someone gets shot some people holler for more gun control instead of learning how to use one in their own defense."

"Suzy," I said. "I've watched you on a number of

occasions, and I have to say that in spite of the fact you were present when your father was shot, and you lost your mother, I've never met anyone who less resembles a victim. There is no victim mentality unless one perceives oneself to be a victim, and you don't think of yourself that way."

"True," she said. "This may sound trite or cold but it's the way I feel. Rather than have them go through some long illness or maybe one die and the survivor live for years without the other, perhaps be in a nursing home or something worse, I'm glad my parents went the way they did. Dad felt a lot of pain but it didn't last long. Mom went out like a light and they went out together. I hate what happened, but Mom died with Dad in her arms and Dad died right after. Fate.

"I'm sorry they weren't at my wedding, I wish they could have been here when my sister had her child and I hate the fact they're never going to hold this baby I'm carrying in their arms. I miss them on a daily basis; their death leaves a gap in my life that can't be filled by anything else. But in many ways, a lot worse things could have happened."

"How do you do it?" I asked. "You're a month or so from having a baby, you're still doing your media work, and you're running for the Texas legislature. Most people would have had their life completely derailed by the kind of thing that happened at Luby's."

She paused and thought for a minute, drawing

an invisible picture on the table with her index finger. Finally she looked up and said, "What I'm going to say may sound incredibly simplistic, but this is the way I see it.

"When something like this occurs there are only two things you can do. You either deal with it, really deal with it, and go on with your life, or you wallow in it and go nuts. Neither one is really all that thrilling, but going on is a whole lot better than whining about it.

"That's all it comes down to."

As Suzie says, that's all it comes down to. The tools to provide you with a certain level of security are at hand. The old saying, "God made all men but Colonel Colt made them equal," applies to women too.

You've read the stories of four women with guns, who fought men for their lives and survived, and you also just read the story of a woman who couldn't carry a gun and because of it a mass murderer killed her parents in front of her eyes. If you knew Suzie like I know Suzie, you'd be as sure as I am that if she'd had her gun in her purse instead of her car her parents and a lot of others would have not died that day. Such a small but vital difference between the quick and the dead.

Suzy had her baby, and won her election. She now represents her district in the Texas House of Representatives. The right to self-defense has no better friend in politics than Representative Suzanna Gratia Hupp of the 54th Legislative District of Texas.

If we'd wanted, we could have included the stories of the forty thousand women who were killed in the last ten years who couldn't or didn't defend themselves. Perhaps retell the Kitty Genovese story. A heart-wrenching case of a woman who was killed in the middle of a New York City street in the full sight of her neighbors, yet no one answered her repeated screams. Ms. Genovese's attacker used a knife. What do you suppose would have happened if Ms. Genovese had had something with which to defend herself—even a firearm?

We could tell the stories of the two million reported rape victims of the last decade, or of the additional two million who didn't report their attack. Or the tens of millions of women who were robbed, mugged, beaten, burglarized, or otherwise victimized by the criminal element. But we don't need to do that. Your local news will tell you all about them. Each and every night. It's up to us to tell the other side of the story.

A gun cannot guarantee your safety any more than the government can, but there is one major difference between the two. When the housebreaker kicks in your door or your crazy ex-boyfriend decides if he can't have you, no one can, you can choose to defend yourself and your children. You can choose whether you have your gun in your hand. Whatever your choice, remember, no one else will be there: not your local police, not the anti–self-defense lobby, not your government.

The stories I included here are of extraordinary courage by women who, before they were confronted by their assailant, were really quite ordinary people. These stories illustrate important lessons—both obvious and not so obvious.

Sammie Foust teaches us never to give up. If at any time during her ordeal she had ceased to fight, even after she'd shot her assailant two or three times, he would have killed her. He almost did anyway. As long as your assailant continues to attack, you continue to fight back. Sammie had only four rounds in her firearm but all four of them ended up in the bad guy. Had it been only two or three, it's doubtful she would have survived.

Never, ever forget that in these circumstances survival is what it's about. If you need to, you can work out that "victim thing" in therapy, after the fact.

Charmaine Klaus tells us that you simply do the best you can in the circumstances. Because she had a weapon and at least had a chance to fight for her life she has escaped the entire victim mentality syndrome. She fought, she put a bullet in her attacker, and even though her friend was killed and she was wounded, her attacker did not prevail. Charmaine sleeps without nightmares because she knows she did the best she could under the circumstances and her attacker did not get away.

Dottie Collins was socially inculturated to be a victim of the abusive male from the day she was born. She grew up without knowing there was another way of life and for most of her life there had been no other way. One who does not have such an experience can in no way appreciate the amount of personal courage and fortitude it took for her to make the moves she's made in her life. Yes, she tells us that a woman has the right to defend herself from an abusive lover, and that's important, even though we should already know that. But the most difficult thing Dottie's done in her life is surviving her environment and developing the mentality that would allow her to decide that she would and could defend her life. That she could rise above the limitations society and lack of education placed upon her is a minor miracle, and should serve as an inspiration to an entire group of women who are in similar situations. We must remember that life is a river, not a frozen lake. It flows from one area to another. The segment of society in which you are born does not have to be the one you stay in—unless that is your choice.

Brenda Hibbitts teaches us to shoot when you have to and don't shoot when you don't have to. The group broke into her house, she ordered them to leave, they did not, and the leader threatened her with a hammer. She shot him to save herself. The object of self-defense is to end the assault against you, not to kill. She allowed the other housebreakers to flee and ultimately let the guy who threatened her do the same. She could have killed the rest of them but chose not to. Brenda took care of business by shooting when she had to, and further took care of business by not shooting when she didn't have to. Because of doing exactly the right thing, Brenda Hibbitts has no resulting guilt and no problems with the legal system.

Suzy Gratia Hupp illustrates both the saddest and most positive examples of citizenship. We see what happens to law-abiding citizens when their government refuses to give them the right to carry a weapon. Then we see what a difference an individual citizen can make, because Texas now has a right-to-carry law and Dr. Suzanna Gratia Hupp is a newly elected member of the state legislature.

These women, their courage and fortitude, and their stories serve to illustrate the following point. A woman with a firearm and the courage to use it is the equal of any criminal, any rapist, any abuser. With a gun and your wits you have a fighting chance. Without one, you're like Blanche DuBois, eternally depending on the kindness of strangers.

Author's Note

The information on laws that appears in the Supplements has been prepared with the editorial assistance of my friend and colleague, Alan Korwin. Alan is a professional author and management consultant. He and coauthor Michael P. Anthony published their book on firearms laws, *Gun Laws of America*, in 1995, which former attorney general of Arizona, Bob Corbin, calls "outstanding." Following the success of *Gun Laws of America*, Alan began publishing his *Gun Owner's Guide* series. As of the beginning of 1997, his publishing company, Bloomfield Press, has published books covering the state gun laws of Arizona, Texas, and Virginia. Bloomfield Press plans to publish several additional compendiums in 1997, with California and Florida at the top of the list. Alan's talents, both conceptually and editorially, I believe, add greatly to the usefulness of *Safe, Not Sorry*.

Supplement 1

THE FUNDAMENTAL RIGHT OF SELF-DEFENSE

Without your own personal safety, little else matters. You can hardly enjoy the pursuit of happiness without some measure of freedom from wanton acts against yourself, your family, or your property. People who would take what is yours or do you harm have unfortunately been around since the dawn of human history, and so have the sensible measures good people take to protect themselves from evil.

Official Protection from Crime

Crime-prevention services from the police are a valuable tool in modern society. They serve an important function, and with the exception of the extreme total disarmament proponents, Americans support their local police. But it is critical to recognize that the police are not legally obligated to protect you personally. Their failure to protect you is not illegal, and you cannot sue them for failing to show up, or for failing to do anything constructive if and when they do respond to your call for help. Not all 911 calls get a police response.

Most people do not know or understand this. The courts, however, have continually and uniformly made this assertion with iron certainty.

Using more than thirty cases to make the point, the standard U.S. legal reference, *American Jurisprudence* (57 Am Jur 2d 441), puts it plainly:

> In the absence of special circumstances, there is no duty resting on a municipality or other governmental body to provide police protection to any particular person and the government may not be held liable for its failure to do so . . .

In a related section (446) it adds, ". . . even where a person has anticipated harm and requested police protection." To do otherwise, it says, would make the government an insurer to all, for the mere act of setting up a police force.

Although certain extreme cases can be tried (the "special circumstances" mentioned), lawsuits brought against the police for failure to respond or failure to act are routinely thrown out of court.

In addition, the ability of the police to stop crime is extremely low, and it's not even their fault. Routine police procedures involve arriving after the fact, securing the scene, drawing chalk lines, collecting evidence, writing reports, and attempting to find criminals who have long since split.

At the time an assault occurs there are usually only two people present: the criminal and the intended victim. The number of crimes in progress that are actually interrupted and thus prevented by the police is tiny. Shockingly, such statistics are not even kept.

So how do police serve you and me? They serve society as a whole, not people as individuals, and that is the only standard to which they are accountable. Quoting *American Jurisprudence* again,

> . . . the duty of providing protection from crime is one owed only to the general public . . . a police department's negligence, its oversights, blunders and omissions, are not the proximate or legal cause of harm committed by others.

Police serve as a crime-deterring visible presence in selected high-profile areas (which basically means that criminals cleverly conduct their activities when and where police are not around). Police serve us admirably during natural disasters and in response to general emergencies, and for traffic and crowd control. And police follow up on crimes . . . it's a rotten job but someone has to do it. They arrest suspected perpetrators after the fact. They break up family fights. Stopping a rape in progress is virtually unheard of.

Which is all the more reason that the right to self-defense is fundamental. The best studies available indicate that firearms are used two and a half million times a year, without even being fired, to prevent criminals from carrying out their deeds. The reason that, as the saying goes, "there is rarely a police officer around when you need one" is because that's when a criminal chooses to victimize you. They may be criminals but they're not fools.

In case you still cling to the notion that the authorities are there to personally protect you, look at the frightening statistics below. There are only fifty states. Some of these incidents, compiled from FBI reports for 1994, happened near you.

Murders the police didn't prevent:	23,305
Reported rapes the police didn't prevent:	102,096
Robberies the police didn't prevent:	618,817
Aggravated assaults the police didn't prevent:	1,119,950
Burglaries the police didn't prevent:	2,712,156
Serious crimes that actually occured:	All of the above
Total crimes the police prevented:	No stats available

Even more shocking are the unsolved crimes, in which the criminals were never identified and are still out there, presumably continuing their criminal affairs (also 1994 figures from the FBI):

Murders with no arrests:	4,808
Rapes with no arrests:	72,305
Robberies with no arrests:	471,838
Aggravated assaults with no arrests:	670,234
Burglaries with no arrests:	2,392,230

And the final nail in the statistical coffin on the effectiveness of official crime protection would seem to be the results. The numbers above show that there are not even arrests in seventy-nine percent of all violent crimes.

And for those unlucky suspects who are finally convicted (U.S. Department of Justice statistics for 1990–91):

Average sentence for a convicted murderer:	20.3 years
Average time a convicted murderer spends in jail:	7.7 years
Average sentence for a convicted rapist:	13.3 years
Average time a rapist spends in jail:	4.6 years
Average sentence for a convicted robber:	9.9 years
Average time a robber spends in jail:	3.3 years
Percentage of paroled convicts rearrested for violent crime:	51%
Violent criminals convicted and serve no jail time:	60,000/year

In other words, you're dead forever and in a few years your murderer is out having a hamburger and a beer. As you can see, the police cannot and do not protect you. Self-defense is your right—your primary civil right.

To sum up the realities of self-defense:

1. Crime is real and the authorities provide limited protection.
2. You always have the choice of defending yourself in an emergency.
3. You have the legal right to defend yourself.
4. You have a moral obligation to your loved ones and your community to protect yourself.
5. When push comes to shove, you will likely be the only person able to protect yourself from harm.

Thomas Jefferson quoted the eminent criminologist Cesare Beccaria on the crux of the issue:

> Laws that forbid the carrying of arms . . . disarm only those who are neither inclined nor determined to commit crimes . . . such laws make things worse for the assaulted and better for the assailants; they serve rather to encourage than to prevent homicides, for an unarmed man may be attacked with greater confidence than an armed man.

Self-Defense Has Always Been Legal

Self-defense is your fundamental civil right. It springs into existence from the simple fact that you are here, and have as much right to be here as anyone else. Without that right, there is no thread from which to weave the fabric of society. Self-defense has existed uninterrupted since the earliest written law nearly four thousand years ago.

The concept of self-defense extends to the defense of your loved ones or other innocents. Many people believe you have a duty to protect your family that exceeds even your responsibility to yourself.

It's not uncommon to hear a woman say she would never attempt to defend herself from a rapist, abuser, or violent criminal. However, when asked about defending her children, this same woman would instantly tear a perpetrator limb from limb with her bare hands if necessary to protect her kids. Our society applauds such mettle. It should be remembered that by protecting yourself you protect your children too. How would the kids fare if you weren't around to raise them?

The personal use of deadly force is also justified when it is necessary for the prevention of certain extreme crimes, such as arson of an occupied building, attempted murder, kidnapping, armed robbery, sexual assault, and more. Although each state has its own laws for the use of physical or deadly force in self-defense, certain basic principles apply across the board.

Whether you have decided to arm yourself or not for personal safety, please get and read the laws on self-defense for your state. Read some of the cases your state courts have decided. Read what the Supreme Court has had to say on the basic principles. A librarian can help you find the books.

If you have decided to take responsibility for your own safety, the safety of your children, or of your loved ones, find an attorney who is knowledgeable in the self-defense laws in your state and schedule a visit. Get some sound advice on what your rights and responsibilities are. Keep the attorney's number handy, because after you have had to defend yourself is the wrong time to go looking for an attorney.

It's critical to recognize, right at the start, that anytime you use force of any kind there are legal risks to you. For this reason alone, this book and plain common sense suggest you avoid whenever possible any situation that will require the use of force. Learn the tactics and strategies for crime avoidance and personal safety as explained in *Safe, Not Sorry*, and make them a part of your life.

If you ever use force, deadly or otherwise, in any situation, you may be subjected to investigation, arrest, and life-threatening legal actions. You may spend time in jail waiting for the authorities to decide what to do with you. Your fate is in someone else's hands; someone who may or may not think that self-defense was the proper way to solve the problem you faced.

When a person who kills another person is put on trial, even in the most pure example of self-defense, the charge by the prosecution will be some form of manslaughter, homicide, or other serious felony. There is no such thing as a self-defense trial; self-defense is merely your claim against being convicted of murder.

As horrible as all that sounds, it is better than being dead, maimed, or crippled at the hands of a criminal. It is better than leaving your grieving loved ones behind. It is better than seeing your loved ones murdered. Killing to survive is an option you want to take only when there are no other options left open to you.

In the most obvious cases of self-defense the authorities can "no-bill" the survivor. This means that, because the defense is self-evident, no arrest is made and no charges are brought. You are innocent and free to get on with the rest of your life. Someone may occasionally suggest you deserve a Medal of Honor.

Self-defense cases have all the attributes of great news stories—crime, violence, victims and survivors, and justice being served. Justifiable homicide happens practically every day in America, as indicated by FBI statistics. But the mainstream news media steadfastly refuse to feature or even report such incidents, preferring instead to feature senseless criminal violence. And in some situations, for reasons all their own, the media may decide to "try" you on the evening news or in the morning paper.

So just what does it take, then, to use deadly force and not be more guilty than your assailant?

The Nine Fundamental Elements of True Self-Defense

Upon hearing these principles, some critics are bound to intone, "You're telling people when they can go out and kill!" That's a gross distortion. This book does not encourage anyone to go out and kill. The law allows anyone to use deadly force to protect innocent life in the most dire emergency, and there's a world of difference. The result may be the same. An aggressive villain may be slain, but the intention of the targeted victim is not to kill but to protect.

The laws are on the books, they are there for a reason, and you have a right to know what the laws are.

1. You must be completely free from any fault when an incident occurs.

If you had any role, no matter how slight, in creating the affray, your protective legal cloak is weakened or eliminated altogether. Provoking a fight and then using it as an excuse to kill is murder. Invitations to "step outside," dueling, and other forms of what the law calls mutual combat leave both parties open to criminal charges, and rightly so.

You must be in a place where you have a right to be, doing nothing illegal, minding your own business, and the attack must be unprovoked by you in any way. The further your situation strays from this, the shakier your claim of self-defense will be. Prosecutors have taken things to extremes by attempting to blame people for being in dangerous locations at late hours. As this book has already suggested, stay away from such areas whenever possible.

There is one case when a person may share some fault in starting an argument but be able to legally defend himself later. This occurs when you withdraw, completely and in good faith, from an incident you helped start, and the other person presses on with the attack after you've clearly attempted to withdraw as far as you reasonably could.

If you have any relationship to an attacker, the issue of your innocence becomes much more complicated. There will obviously be circumstances that must be examined if a confrontation involves your parents, spouse, children, in-laws, boss, coworker, neighbor, friend, teacher, grocer, or drinking buddy. It is tragic how many homicides involve people who know each other. It is also a warning that mortal threats often come from people you know. Knowing your assailant can make an event much less likely to be a pure case of self-defense, and more likely a case of criminal assault or homicide.

Examples of faultlessness:
You are at home when a stranger breaks in; you are walking down a public street in broad daylight when accosted and assaulted by a stranger.

Examples of possibly sharing part of the fault in the eyes of the court or jury:
The attacker is someone you don't like, have fought with before, or who irritates you; you have unsettled business with the assailant.

Related Supreme Court cases: *Beard v. United States,*

1895; *Rowe v. United States,* 1896; *Brown v. United States,* 1921.

2. You must reasonably believe you are in a life-threatening situation.

It is not enough to be in fear for your life or limb, there must be reasonable grounds to have such a fear. Something must exist that gives grounds to your fear, or your actions will be seen as paranoid or unwarranted. No amount of being legitimately afraid is sufficient without a basis for the fear.

Everything can hinge on this admittedly flexible notion of reasonableness. There are differences between how reasonable your actions are and how reasonable you or another person might think they are. Some states try to determine how reasonable you thought the actions were at the critical moment. Others ask how reasonable it would seem to someone else in the same situation (which in effect means your jury members).

Examples of grounds for reasonable belief:

A person accosts you with a weapon in hand; a stranger breaks into your home and comes after you.

Examples of grounds for belief that may not be reasonable:

You hear worrisome sounds on the other side of a door; you see a group of menacing-looking people on the street.

Related Supreme Court cases: *Beard v. United States,* 1895; *Acers v. United States,* 1896; *Alberty v. United States,* 1896; *Allen v. United States,* 1896; *Wallace v. United States,* 1896.

3. There must be an overt threatening act. Words alone are never enough.

Believing someone will attack is not enough. Someone who swears they will kill you, without actually doing something, does not justify your use of any force. The person must take some deliberate action indicating a true threat. Someone holding a knife, club, or even a gun may or may not justify lethal action on your part; the weapon must be presented in a way that you would reasonably perceive as manifestly and seriously dangerous to your life or limb.

Examples of overt threatening acts:

A person reaches to draw a gun; a person raises a weapon as if to bring it into use; a person attempts to grapple with you.

Examples of potential threats that do not involve overt acts:

You see someone wearing a sidearm; a person walks to a vehicle where a weapon might be.

Related Supreme Court cases: *Allison v. United States*, 1895; *Acers v. United States*, 1896; *Alberty v. United States*, 1896; *Allen v. United States*, 1896.

4. Necessity must exist.

The legal concept of necessity means that your defensive actions are immediately required. There is no time for you to wait. The legal protection for acting with lethal force exists only at the exact moment of danger, while *necessity* is present, not before and not after. If even the slightest wait would immediately put you in jeopardy of death or serious bodily injury, necessity exists. If you believe you could still safely wait a moment before acting, then you've acted too soon, before the threat was real, making your actions illegal. The instant the danger is over, necessity ends and the right to use deadly force in self-defense evaporates.

Examples of necessity:

You point a gun at an attacker, say, "Don't come any closer," and the person keeps coming, even if slowly; an advancing stranger lifts a knife as if to stab you.

Examples where necessity does not exist:

You point a gun at an attacker, say, "Don't come any closer," and the person stays put; you encounter an intruder at your door who, on seeing you, runs out the door.

Related Supreme Court cases: *Beard v. United States,* 1895; *Rowe v. United States,* 1896.

5. Only equal force may be used.

When using force to defend yourself, you may not exceed the amount of force being used or threatened against you. If you use more force than you are confronted with, then you become the aggressor, the other person is the victim, and you have probably given up any claim of self-defense. This is often expressed as hand for hand, stick for stick, weapon for weapon, but it is much more complex than that.

Hand for hand between a frail person and a weight lifter, or between one person and four adversaries, is not an even match. The frail person or lone defender might be justified in the use, or at least the threatened use, of some weapon against such a hand. There are lots of shades of gray here, which may be settled later in a courtroom.

Bringing deadly force to bear, if not clearly in response to an equally deadly threat, is risky from a legal standpoint. Even though a punch can actually kill, or cause the loss of an eye or an organ, or result in other permanent damage (serious bodily injury, in legal terms), it is nearly impossible to predict the damage such a blow might cause. Using lethal force in defense against a punch therefore can be difficult to support in court.

This is a difficult concept for many people, and does put an honest citizen in an awkward position. If a person deliberately and with hostile intent hits you in the knee with a baseball bat you could be crippled for life, but it's practically impossible to know this beforehand. You might be justified in shooting such an assailant while he's swinging. But how could you possibly demonstrate the extent of the threat after your shot has stopped the swing?

The best strategy in such a situation may be avoidance, as is so often the case. Step out of the way of the blow, defuse the situation before the blow, remove yourself from the scene altogether. What were you doing there in the first place, the prosecution will ask.

Using the threat of a weapon to deter the blow is a possibility, but now you've threatened gun against stick. This may not hold up weeks after the incident in a court of law.

And yet, if witnesses were present and agree that the bat wielder was belligerent and you were conciliatory, your chances improve dramatically. Were there witnesses? Who are they and what will they say? Every incident must be judged by its own unique set of circumstances.

Examples that are likely to be seen as equal force:

Someone pushes you and you push back, someone tries to stab you in the chest and you shoot back.

Examples that may be seen as unequal force:

Someone pushes you and you hit him with a stick; someone threatens you verbally and you hit him; someone slaps you in the face and you draw a gun.

Related Supreme Court cases: *Beard v. United States*, 1895; *Alberty v. United States*, 1896; *Allen v. United States*, 1896.

6. Once the threat is over the right to use deadly force ends.

You may use deadly force in defense only while life and limb are immediately and illegally in jeopardy. The instant the threat stops you must hold your fire. If an assailant is down from one or multiple gunshot wounds, you may not continue firing unless they still pose some real threat. If the person still holds a gun or is trying to bring it to bear, the threat may still exist. Walking over and shooting an incapacitated attacker is most likely murder.

Related Supreme Court cases: *Acers v. United States*, 1896; *Brown v. United States*, 1921.

7. It is very risky to chase a criminal who is leaving the scene.

It is generally unwise for a private citizen to pursue a criminal who is fleeing the scene of a crime. When the confrontation ends, give thanks for surviving and let it end. If you go after the criminal, you might legally become the attacker yourself. Pursuit is not self-defense. In a bizarre but logical turn of circumstance, the criminal could now defend against your attack and claim self-defense. Don't laugh, it's happened. Attempting a so-called citizen's arrest, unless you really know what you're doing, should probably be avoided. If all that occurred was the theft of some of your property, any attempt to kill in response is wholly unjustified.

8. You may have a "duty to retreat."

Some states make it mandatory that, before you can legally use deadly force, you make every reasonable effort to safely withdraw from a confrontation. You must be backed against a wall with nowhere left to go, so to speak, before you can bring down an attacker. Whether your state requires this or not, it makes logical, legal, and moral sense to do this. Take any steps possible to avoid having to take the life of another human being. A prosecutor will do everything possible to point out if you could have ducked or stepped back and instead willfully chose to shoot down a person, no matter how evil you believe the person was. The duty to retreat, if required, is tempered by your safe ability to do so. If retreat would put you at risk, or increase your risk, it is virtually impossible for a court to require it.

In contrast, some states allow you to stand your ground in the face of a deadly attack, and even if escape might be possible, to return fire or otherwise lethally ward off a life-threatening attack.

Chief Justice Oliver Wendell Holmes put it elegantly in the 1921 Supreme Court case of *Brown v. United States*, when he said, "Detached reflection cannot be demanded in the presence of an uplifted knife."

In addition, the duty to retreat generally does not apply in your own home in many states. The so-called castle doctrine makes your home an extension of yourself, and your latitude to act in your own defense in your home is typically greater than for an event that occurs out in public.

When the police arrive, the fact that you're the homeowner, and the victim is a stranger (or even wanted on other charges, or a repeat offender released from custody) is usually clear evidence in your favor. Retreat from your own home would mean giving up your residence to a criminal perpetrator who invades it, and is hard to justify in a civilized society. The Supreme Court stands quite vigorously on this point.

There was one notable exception, though. One state's law used to require you to turn your home over to an attacker and leave, rather than defend against the attack, if you could safely get out. Abandoning your home is always an option, and might well be the best tactic in a given situation. But to be forced by the government to abandon your own home when under attack? What can you say about a legal system where a criminal's right to be in your home is greater than your own. The law was repealed.

Related Supreme Court cases: *Beard v. United States*, 1895; *Alberty v. United States*, 1896; *Rowe v. United States*, 1896; *Brown v. United States*, 1921.

9. *Your intent must be just.*

Your goal isn't to kill. It is to survive. Only while and only because your actual survival is at stake may you act with lethal power.

Related Supreme Court cases: *Gourko v. United States*, 1894; *Thompson v. United States*, 1894; *Allen v. United States*, 1896; *Wallace v. United States*, 1896.

SUPPLEMENT 2

HOW THE FEDERAL GUN LAWS AFFECT YOU

It is a pretty common misconception that federal laws are somehow "higher" or more important than your state's laws. Federal laws aren't more potent than state laws; they cover different things. Except for the Constitution, which provides the overriding rules that everyone is supposed to operate under, the control exercised by Washington and the lawmaking of your own state are in large measure separate. Lawyers would say they have *differing jurisdiction*.

For example, federal law controls the method and number of firearms imported to the United States. The states have nothing to do with the process, and exercise no control, except perhaps for minor details at the port where overseas shipments actually arrive. Federal laws—and rooms of regulations authorized by those laws—have established the rules, paperwork, taxation, and controls on imported firearms and ammunition. In addition, federal laws govern the manufacture, distribution, and sales of American-made firearms.

The states, on the other hand, control the enforcement

of laws on self-defense and crime prevention. There are no "justifiable homicide" statutes on the federal books. But every state in the union has these self-defense laws (or relies on common law and history). If it ever comes down to whether your use of deadly force was allowable under law, the law of the state, not any federal authority, determines your fate.

Now, of course, there's a little more gray to it than that. The jurisdiction of federal and state laws may sometimes overlap, or the authorities may think they overlap and fight amongst themselves over who has jurisdiction. The Supreme Court is the ultimate arbiter in whether a given law is constitutional and enforceable, or if official proceedings have properly protected your rights. National civil rights laws can be used if a person's civil rights have been jeopardized. If a criminal act occurs in federal domain but there is no federal law against it, then state law is used to define the crime (according to the Assimilative Crimes Act of 1948).

Federal laws may seem more awesome because all fifty states are affected in one stroke of the pen. Actions at the state level almost never approach the impact that federal laws have on the country as a whole. But as a citizen, you are personally affected by both federal and state laws. You must comply with all, regardless of their source.

Indian reservations may be the most confusing places for determining who is in charge. A non-Indian caught in a firearm violation in Indian Country may be tossed between federal, state, county, Indian, and Bureau of Indian Affairs authorities.

For the most part, regular citizens can count on state

laws (or laws of localities within the states, such as counties or cities) to regulate carrying and use of firearms where they live. Fundamental controls on the firearm itself originate from Congress, a policy that began with the National Firearms Act of 1934.

Gun Regulation in America Today

GENERALLY UNDER FEDERAL CONTROLS	GENERALLY UNDER STATE CONTROLS
Manufacture	Self-Defense
Importation	Crime Prevention
Interstate Shipping	Use of Deadly Force
Collecting	Carrying
Minimum Ages	Minimum Ages, Including Hunting
Prohibited Weapons	Prohibited Weapons
Dealer Licenses	Commercial Zoning Ordinances
Citizen Paperwork	Resident Paperwork
Terrorist Acts	Criminal Acts
Interstate Transportation	Roads
Airlines & Commercial Carriers	Rivers and Lakes
Prohibited Possessors	Prohibited Possessors
Federal Lands	State and Private Lands
School Zones	School Grounds
Federal Facilities	Concealed-Weapon Licensing
Military Arms	Police Arms
Taxation	Taxation

Federal gun laws have grown by more than ninety percent in the last fifty years, with seventy-five percent of that growth since 1960 alone—and they continue to grow. In the first half of 1996, federal gun law grew by an additional ten percent, with passage of the Firearms Safety Act and the Terrorism Act, despite congressional assurances of a gun-law moratorium. Many people have become skeptical of claims that additional gun laws will help stem social and crime problems in the country. The total now stands at 82,855 words of federal gun law. No equivalent figures are available for the states.

It is interesting to note that no federal statutes governing firearms are on the books from the first 128 years of this country's history. Somehow, in the early years, we got by mainly on the Bill of Rights. In fact, the very first federal gun laws actually required people to keep arms.

No, the 232 federal gun statutes are recent inventions, attempted cures for the criminal problems of modern times. At this point, anything even remotely criminal about gun possession and use has been outlawed, and strangely, the crime problems of modern times continue to grow. The truth of the matter is that *gun laws aren't related to how many criminals there are or why they do what they do.*

The first modern federal firearms statute was the 1934 National Firearms Act. This Act was a direct result of criminal gang activity using machine guns. When the Eighteenth Amendment to the Constitution, prohibiting "the manufacture, sale, or transportation of intoxicating liquors . . . for beverage purposes," was ratified in 1919, a new criminal industry was launched. For the next decade and a half, bloody wars over the distribution and sale of illegal liquor were fought. You've seen the movies.

After the Eighteenth Amendment was repealed in 1933, the federal government decided to regulate the sale and transfer of machine guns and other weapons in gangsters' arsenals, using tax law to avoid the strict constitutional rule against infringement.

In 1968 it was political assassinations that propelled Congress, relying on its interstate commerce powers, to institute the wide-ranging controls on every facet of firearm manufacture, distribution, sale, and possession that are in place today.

Prior to the 1968 Gun Control Act, and even though people routinely bought firearms through the mail, at department stores, and at local shops, crime was not the wildly violent random madness it is today. Kids took .22 caliber rifles to school so they could compete on the rifle team, while during hunting season it was not unusual for a long gun or two to be placed in the corner of the classroom, for use after the bell. Violence with those guns by schoolchildren was nonexistent and unthinkable.

When we look to the laws as the reason for or solution to crime, we are looking in the wrong place. What the laws have done is kept all the honest folks in line—the potential victims who read books like these in order to protect themselves and avoid arrest.

The onrush of new gun laws has been matched so steadily by the burgeoning crush of crime that we could ask if crime may be caused by the proliferation of gun laws. The solution, I would suggest, is *not* more gun laws.

The Main Federal Gun Laws

Second, Fourth, and Ninth Amendments from the Bill of Rights (1791)

The Second Amendment to the Constitution guarantees the right to bear arms. Our founding fathers, from Thomas Jefferson to James Madison to Samuel Adams, believed that the Constitution should guarantee arms to citizens. As Samuel Adams said, "The Contitution shall never be construed to authorize Congress to prevent the people of the United States, who are peaceable citizens, from keeping their own arms."

The Fourth Amendment, not often thought of as a firearm right, prohibits the government from taking anything you own without due process of law (and even then, not without compensation, guaranteed under the Fifth Amendment), including firearms.

The lonely and overlooked Ninth Amendment, in an elegant solution to the founding fathers' concerns that they might have missed something, guarantees Americans any rights that exist that aren't listed. The Ninth serves to protect the right to keep and bear arms too.

Fourteenth Amendment to the Constitution (1868)

Slaves were freed after the Civil War, but that doesn't mean they were free. States concocted some pretty elaborate schemes to keep former slaves under control, and a significant effort was made to prevent them from arming themselves. Many of the roots of gun control policy trace directly back to efforts to disarm freed slaves.

Congress responded with the Fourteenth Amendment, which prohibits states from denying citizens their rights as Americans. The Supreme Court has been vigorous in applying the Fourteenth Amendment to Bill of Rights guarantees, though the specific issue of firearms has not yet come to the high court. Your state, if it severely restricts your right to bear arms, may have violated the Fourteenth Amendment guarantee, and a case could eventually wind up on the Court's calendar.

National Firearms Act (1934)

This represents the first national effort at infringing on the right to keep and bear arms by the federal government. Nothing like it had ever been tried before. Using its power to levy taxes, Congress placed detailed registration controls on a group of weapons that have become known by the law's acronym, NFA weapons. To own an NFA weapon today (a machine gun or short shotgun for example) you must be cleared by the FBI, fingerprinted, registered, and the weapon itself is also registered. Although radical from a historical perspective, the law had low initial impact on the population in general.

In 1938 the Federal Firearms Act modified this law slightly and added explosives to the items under control.

Gun Control Act (1968)

This is the law that currently regulates most private gun activity. When you stroll into a gun shop on a nice sunny day, the entire transaction falls under federal regulations that were instituted by this Act. Other laws have added to the controls over the years, and most of these can be found under the Title 18 of federal law, *Crimes and Criminal Procedure.*

Under this law, every gun dealer is federally licensed and every sale is recorded by the dealer. All purchasers must provide ID and fill out a form, under penalty of perjury, certifying that they are not prohibited from possessing firearms under federal law. A list of *prohibited possessors* is established (the list appears at the end of this section). All the elements of interstate shipments of firearms are regulated, and detailed record keeping is established.

The statute also prohibits any interstate transfers of handguns, even among family members. Such transfers must take place between licensed dealers, who keep records of the activity. The law goes on to regulate many things that don't apply directly to most citizens, involving importation, manufacture, research, collecting, and more.

With the exception of theft of guns from a dealer's inventory, most GCA crimes are victimless, involving paperwork violations, license irregularities, and possession of arms that don't match legal requirements. All these violations are serious, however, and can have serious consequences to the dealer as well as the buyer. For the most part, GCA violations require actions that are taken knowingly or willfully.

Firearms Owners' Protection Act (1986)

Congress passed this law because infringements on the rights of citizens were getting out of hand. Government agents were harassing dealers and gun-owning citizens who were not committing crimes, for minor and even nonexistent paperwork irregularities. This Act made numerous adjustments to the 1968 law to prevent such abuses and curb government activities.

This law was never assigned a statute number, making it very difficult to find on the books, but we have included the title and congressional findings here:

(a) Short Title.—This Act may be cited as the "Firearms Owners' Protection Act."
(b) Congressional Findings.—
   The Congress finds that—
   (1) the rights of citizens—
      (A) to keep and bear arms under the second amendment to the United States Constitution;
      (B) to security against illegal and unreasonable searches and seizures under the fourth amendment;
      (C) against uncompensated taking of property, double jeopardy, and assurance of due process of law under the fifth amendment; and
      (D) against unconstitutional exercise of authority under the ninth and tenth amendments; require additional legislation to correct existing firearms statutes and enforcement policies; and
   (2) additional legislation is required to reaffirm the intent of the Congress, as expressed in section 101 of the Gun Control Act of 1968, that **"it is not the purpose of this title to place any undue or unnecessary Federal restrictions or burdens on law-abiding citizens with respect to the acquisition, possession, or use of firearms appropriate to the purpose of hunting, trap-shooting,**

target shooting, personal protection, or any other lawful activity, and that this title is not intended to discourage or eliminate the private ownership or use of firearms by law-abiding citizens for lawful purposes (emphasis added)."

Federal Firearms Transportation Guarantee

Part of the Firearms Owners' Protection Act set up this statutory guarantee to all Americans. Basically, if a gun is legal where you start and legal where you finish, it's legal to transport it to and from, unloaded, in the trunk of your car. The title of the law refers to *interstate transportation*, but the law itself makes no such distinction. This law doesn't help much when it comes to personal safety or self-defense, but it is a step in the right direction, and does not increase crime while it ensures citizens a degree of freedom that the government has no power to restrict.

Some state officials have sworn they won't abide by this law, and one man in New Jersey was arrested and convicted (he didn't appeal) regardless of this protective law. Here is Section 926As:

Notwithstanding any other provision of any law or any rule or regulation of a State or any political subdivision thereof, any person who is not otherwise prohibited by this chapter from transporting, shipping, or receiving a firearm shall be entitled to transport a firearm for any lawful purpose from any place where he may lawfully possess and carry such firearm to any other place where he may lawfully possess and carry such firearm if, during such transportation the firearm is unloaded, and neither the firearm nor any ammunition being transported is readily accessible or is directly accessible from the passenger compartment of such transporting vehicle: Provided, That in the case of a vehicle without a compartment separate from the driver's compartment the firearm or ammunition shall be contained in a locked container other than the glove compartment or console.

Brady Handgun Violence Prevention Act (1993)

The Brady Act was approved by Congress in November 1993 and signed into law by President Clinton. The Act requires some states to implement a waiting period of up to five state or government business days for the purchase of a handgun from a federally licensed firearms dealer, and introduces new paperwork requirements on buyers and sellers.

The Brady Law allows anyone with a proper carry permit to make firearm purchases without delays. It also authorizes $200 million a year for the implementation of a federal computer system to instantly check all gun buyers by November 1998. This system, commonly known as the Instant National Criminal Background Check, enables the gun seller to compare the purchaser against a national database of known prohibited persons. If the buyer is not prohibited, the purchase could be instantly consummated; if the purchaser is a prohibited person, the sale cannot be made and an arrest can be instantly effectuated. Brady also regulates certain aspects of shipping firearms by air when you travel, and has some other features. It is lengthy, and may be the most convoluted federal gun statute on the books.

During the waiting period, the chief law enforcement officer (CLEO), who can be a sheriff, police chief, or other official in the buyer's area, "shall make a reasonable effort" to determine if the buyer is prohibited from purchasing a handgun. If the CLEO believes the buyer needs the handgun for self-protection or to protect a member of his/her household, the sale may be approved immediately as well.

When the law was passed, eighteen states were exempt. Since then, ten more states have established an instant check system or have otherwise modified their laws to become exempt from the Brady provisions. As a result, fewer than half the states are subject to Brady delays and paperwork.

At the same time that the Bureau of Alcohol, Tobacco and Firearms announced that forty-four thousand people had been initially (not necessarily finally) stopped from a retail handgun purchase (which is a five-year federal felony if convicted), President Clinton announced a sixty thousand figure, and Sarah Brady announced one hundred thousand (the last two at the Democratic Presidential Convention). Unfortunately the number of Justice Department prosecutions of all these felons who provided us with their names, addresses, and signatures, has been only seven.

Public Safety and Recreational Firearms Use Protection Act (1994)

Popularized as the Crime Bill, it puts a ten-year moratorium on the manufacture and importation of certain types of firearms and accessories for the general public. It does not affect the possession or transfer of those items that were lawfully possessed on or before the enactment date of September 13, 1994. This law has also (erroneously) been called the "assault weapons ban."

The act defines certain firearms as "assault weapons" by either name or description. All in all, the law affects more than 175 semiautomatic rifles, pistols, and shotguns. In addition, this law prohibits the possession or transfer of a new "large capacity ammunition feeding device," which in English means newly made magazines with a greater than ten-shot capacity. No existing firearms or accessories were banned, and it is perfectly legal to buy, sell, own, and use any of the affected weapons that existed before passage of the act. This prohibition impacted gun makers in a way the writers of the legislation never anticipated: Companies now make handguns that are smaller, more concealable, and much more practical in the modern world.

Rifle Practice and Firearms Safety Act (1996)

The Civilian Marksmanship Program, run by the U.S. Army, has served as the federal government's official firearms training, supply, and competitions program for U.S. citizens since 1956. Its history traces back to the late 1800s, when programs were first established to help ensure that the populace could shoot straight, in the event an army had to be raised to defend the country. The program is privatized by this Act.

The federal government transfers the responsibility and facilities for training civilians in the use of small arms to a 501(c)(3) nonprofit corporation created for this purpose. All law-abiding citizens are eligible to participate, and priority is given to reaching and training youth in the safe, lawful, and accurate use of firearms.

Functions formerly performed for this program by the Army are now the responsibility of this new corporation. The Army is required to provide direct support and to take whatever action is necessary to make the program work in its privatized form. The stated program goals are:

1. Teaching marksmanship to U.S. citizens.
2. Promoting practice and safety in the use of firearms.
3. Conducting matches and competitions.
4. Awarding trophies and prizes.
5. Procuring supplies and services needed for the program.
6. Securing and accounting for all firearms, ammunition, and supplies used in the program.
7. Giving, lending, or selling firearms, ammunition, and supplies under the program.
8. Priority must be given to training youths, and reaching as many youths as possible.

Any person who is not a felon, hasn't violated the main federal gun laws, and does not belong to a group that advocates violent overthrow of the U.S. government may participate in the Civilian Marksmanship Program.

Omnibus Consolidated Appropriations Act (1997)—Gun Free School Zones

Congress was stopped in its attempt to exercise police powers at the state level in 1995, when the U.S. Supreme Court declared the 1991 Gun-Free School Zone law unconstitutional. That law was reenacted, to the surprise of many observers, in a form essentially identical to the one the Supreme Court overturned, as an unnoticed add-on to a two-thousand-page federal spending bill.

The law makes it a federal crime to knowingly have a firearm within a thousand feet of any school. An exemption is granted to anyone willing to register with the government for a specified license to carry the firearm, and the prohibition does not apply to: (1) Firearms while on private property that is not part of the school grounds; (2) Any firearm that is unloaded and in a locked container; (3) Any firearm unloaded and locked in a firearms rack on a motor vehicle; (4) Possession of a firearm for use in an approved school program; (5) Possession under a contract with the school; (6) Possession by law enforcement officers in an official capacity; and (7) An unloaded firearm, while crossing school premises to public or private land open to hunting, if crossing the grounds is authorized by the school.

It is also illegal to fire a gun (or attempt to fire a gun), knowingly or with reckless disregard for safety, in a place you know is a school zone, with the following exceptions: (1) On private property that is not part of the school grounds; (2) As part of a program approved by the school; (3) Under contract with the school; (4) By law enforcement acting in an official capacity. Self-defense is not mentioned. States are not prohibited from passing their own laws.

America had 121,855 public and private schools as of 1994. In effect, this law may criminalize the actions of nearly anyone who travels in a populated area with a legally possessed firearm. As with its overturned predecessor, its effect on the very real problem of youth violence is unclear, and of course, any firearm used illegally in America, whether it is near a school or not, is already a serious crime with heavy penalties.

Omnibus Consolidated Appropriations Act (1997)— Misdemeanor Gun Ban for Domestic Violence Offense

Anyone convicted of a state or federal misdemeanor involving the use or attempted use of physical force, or the threatened use of a deadly weapon, against a family member (spouse, parent, guardian, cohabiter, coparent, or similar) is prohibited from possessing a firearm under federal law. This marks the first time that a misdemeanor offense has served as grounds for denial of the constitutional right to keep and bear arms.

No provision is made for the firearms such men and women might already possess. Firearm possession by a prohibited possessor is a five-year federal felony.

A number of narrow conditions may exempt a person from this law, including whether they were represented by an attorney, the type of trial and plea, an expungement or set-aside, or a pardon or other restoration of civil rights.

The law applies equally to law enforcement officers, the armed forces, and agencies like the CIA, FBI, Secret Service, and others. The law is being applied retroactively, and has created a furor across the country, where it may have made criminals of millions of people.

The Main Federal Requirements on Gun Sales and Possession

1. All firearms dealers must be licensed by the Treasury Department and keep records of their sales.
2. You must be at least eighteen years of age to buy a long gun (a rifle or shotgun) or long-gun ammunition from a licensed dealer. You must be at least twenty-one to buy a handgun and matching ammunition from a licensed dealer.
3. When purchasing a firearm from a dealer, you must provide government-issued identification (typically a driver's license, or state ID card issued in lieu of a license).
4. All buyers must fill out a federal form 4473. This requires your name and address, height, weight, race, sex, and date and place of birth. It describes the firearm and its serial number, and includes questions you must answer (listed at the end of this section), under penalty of perjury, that identify people who are prohibited from purchasing firearms.
5. If you are purchasing a handgun, your ID must include a photo, and you must also fill out a federal Brady paperwork form F 5300.35, which is similar to the 4473 form. The Brady information is provided to local law enforcement officials, who conduct a criminal history background check on you before your purchase. At least twenty-eight states have set up instant telephone checks or other systems so you can be cleared while you're at the store and the check may also exempt you from the additional paper-

work. Residents in states that aren't exempt from Brady must wait up to five business days (or more at the state's option; California requires ten, and Tennessee, fifteen) before you can receive your purchases.

In addition, a valid handgun-carry permit typically exempts you completely from all Brady paperwork and delays.

6. To be legal, a rifle must have a barrel more than sixteen inches long, a shotgun barrel must be at least eighteen inches long, and either firearm must be at least twenty-six inches in length overall. Modern long guns meet these requirements, and it is illegal to cut down a long gun to less than these lengths without prior federal authorization.

7. Federal law in 1994 (part of the Public Safety Act) outlawed the possession of handguns or handgun ammunition by anyone under eighteen years of age (purchase was already illegal). Some carefully defined exceptions apply. A minor may have a handgun while carrying written consent from a parent or guardian (who is not a prohibited possessor): (1) In the course of employment; (2) In legitimate ranching or farming; (3) For target practice; (4) For hunting; (5) For a class in the safe and lawful use of a handgun; or (6) For transport, unloaded in a locked case, directly to and from such activities. Also excluded is a minor who uses a handgun against an intruder, at home or in another home where the minor is an invited guest. If a handgun or ammunition is legally transferred to a minor who then commits an offense with the firearm, the firearm must be returned to its lawful owner after legal procedures are concluded. Minors may inherit title to (but not possession) of

a handgun. Except in the cases above, it is illegal to provide a handgun or handgun ammunition to a minor.

The Federal Prohibited Possessor List

Federal law prohibits gun purchase or possession by anyone who:

1. Is charged with or has been convicted of a crime which carries more than a one-year sentence (except for state misdemeanors with up to a two-year sentence);
2. Is a fugitive from justice;
3. Unlawfully uses or is addicted to marijuana, a depressant, a stimulant, or a narcotic drug;
4. Has been adjudicated as a mental defective or mentally incompetent;
5. Is committed to a mental institution;
6. Is an illegal alien;
7. Has been dishonorably discharged from the armed forces;
8. Has renounced U.S. citizenship;
9. Is under a court order restraining harassment, stalking, or threatening of an intimate partner or partner's child;
10. Has been convicted of a domestic violence misdemeanor.

Federal form 4473 phrases these conditions as questions. A "yes" answer to any of the questions disqualifies you from purchase. Filling out the form falsely carries a five-year federal felony sentence. The completed form is stored by the dealer and no copies are made. (State paperwork may also be required.)

SUPPLEMENT 3

HOW YOUR STATE GUN LAWS AFFECT YOU

State law is where the rubber meets the road for those Americans who want to buy, possess, and carry firearms for lawful purposes. The day-to-day issues of purchasing, owning, or carrying a gun on your person, in your car, at work, or at home are controlled by your state laws and local statutes. Your legal protections (and legal risks) in a self-defense altercation spring from your state's attitudes, court system, law enforcement and laws. Most everything that would happen to you if you had to defend yourself from a violent attack would be according to laws of the state in which the incident occurred.

The restrictions and regulations decreed by your state statutes determine how you as a law-abiding citizen can own, carry, or use a firearm. It makes sense for honest gun owners and would-be gun owners who want to avoid inadvertently violating some obscure law to know their state laws.

Of course it makes sense, but it has become virtually

impossible in America. The laws are so vast, interwoven, complex, hard to find, poorly written, and change so much, that getting to know and understand them in any real sense is a full-time job. You have a right to know your laws, but that right is almost impossible to exercise. The situation is outrageous.

Gun law advice from local authorities is sketchy at best and often grossly inaccurate. And someone's word on the telephone just doesn't hold any water should you be thrust before a court.

So unless you have a real passion for long legal tracts, you must face the fact that your knowledge and your attorney's knowledge of the law is going to be less than perfect. Does this mean you can't and shouldn't defend yourself?

No. As a law-abiding citizen of the community, you act honorably, ethically and in good conscience, and trust that truth shall prevail. It often does.

What State Laws Regulate Purchase, Possession, and People Who Are Prohibited from Firearms Ownership

States' statutes spell out these requirements in greater detail than do federal ones. As a matter of fact, most states have laws that are similar to the federal laws on these subjects, as described in Supplement 2. No state can reduce the age restrictions, or other federal restrictions, or change the list of those criminals who are prohibited from owning firearms; but states can, and almost always do, regulate the carrying of firearms.

States have introduced a diverse number of permitting,

licensing, and registration schemes for firearms and for people who bear arms. A few select states and municipalities have their own lists of prohibited firearms, and an even smaller group have literally outlawed the possession of specific firearms. If you live in one of these spots—say, Morton Grove, Illinois—and you're attacked by an armed madman, you can fight back—but you cannot use a handgun. In contrast, Kennesaw, Georgia, requires every home to keep a loaded gun. As you can see, laws vary from state to state and even from town to town.

When you want to purchase a firearm there are some basic federal requirements. The federal 4473 form must be filled out, and false statements turn you into an instant felon. Presently in twenty-two states you must wait an additional five days according to the Brady Law for any handgun sales. Another thirteen states have the preferable Instant Check and Arrest system, where you fill out a form, show your driver's license, and within minutes you are checked by the state's criminal computer check system against the list of people prohibited from owning or purchasing a firearm. If you are a law abiding citizen, you walk out with your handgun.

Other regulations, if any, are directly from your state or community, which may seek to license you, the sale, the gun, carrying it, or a combination of these. You may find three or more forms to fill out, and local waiting periods may apply. If you relocate, expect to find a different process.

If you're a law-abiding citizen with no criminal past, with the exception of New York City, Washington, D.C., and some other localities, you pretty much still have the right to go buy yourself a firearm—but in over seventy percent of the states you will have to wait.

Just don't be surprised when, in the more urbanized and crime-prone chunks of America, you run into well-intentioned bureaucrats and elected officers who run roughshod over your rights in the name of any elusive goal. I had a friend who was a theater professor at the University of Connecticut, who believed that laws restricting the ownership and carrying of firearms served the public interest. He didn't even relate those laws to the constitutional issues they could pose.

One day he was producing a play that required several guns as props, and knowing of my interest in firearms, he called and asked me to find several different firearms for his production. I first explained that I did not own all the guns that he wanted and doubted that he would find anyone to loan him all the guns he needed. Additionally, if he carried these firearms from his home in one town to the neighboring university town, he would be in violation of state and local laws. He was aghast. He stated indignantly that he was not a criminal and had no intention of harming anyone, he only wanted the production of his play to be authentic. I agreed with his noble purposes, but patiently explained that restrictive gun laws only burden the law-abiding. Criminals ignore them any time they please.

Carrying a Gun with You

Federal laws generally do not apply to carrying a gun in your state as long as you legally own the firearm and you're not on federal land (or under federal jurisdiction in places such as airports, nuclear facilities, federal buildings, or school zones). Your state autonomously controls the rules for carrying a gun, literally, for "bearing arms."

Many people believe that this conflicts with the Second Amendment guarantee to bear arms. Indeed, some states have imposed pretty stringent restrictions on their residents, even though the Fourteenth Amendment clearly prohibits individual states from denying the rights of any American citizen. For now, the states have set their own rules, and if you violate any, you face jail terms, fines, and get all the benefits of a police record. A felony conviction erases your right to legally bear arms on a nearly permanent basis.

The many, many differing gun-carry laws are where interstate travelers get into trouble. Even if they know their rules at home, that knowledge is worthless when they step across the border (or in some cases across county lines, or even city boundaries).

How bad can it be, you ask? In Arizona you can put a loaded gun in your glove box. Perfectly legal, everyone does it, keeps the gun reasonably accessible yet discreetly out of sight, and the glove box need not be locked. Drive ten feet across the border into California and you've committed two crimes: You have a gun that's loaded and you have an accessible gun (even if it isn't loaded).

In Texas, for the past 124 years, simply having a handgun on your person has been grounds for arrest. Most Texans are aware of this, though very few outsiders are—they all think Texas is still the Wild West. After your arrest, you're allowed to plead your innocence through a very thin window of allowable excuses, called affirmative defenses. Few people make such a defense, including those who try the "I'm a traveler" excuse in the law, which allows no detours, no extended stops, and expires as soon as you arrive at your distant destination.

The 1995 Texas right-to-carry law, which passed with the support of many Texas women including Suzanne Gratia Hupp, has changed that situation. Today 115,000 Texans, the largest number in the first year of right-to-carry permit issuance, have concealed-carry permits. A survey done of applicants for carry permits showed that the median age was forty-seven years old with nineteen percent between eighteen and thirty-four and twenty-nine percent over fifty-five. In addition, twenty-eight percent of the applicants were women.

Open vs. Concealed Carry

There are two ways to carry a gun under state laws: in plain sight, often called "open carry," or concealed from sight. The option of how to carry a firearm is left to the gun owner in more than one-third of the states. With a logic that eludes people today, some states allow only "open carry" for handguns, so that everyone will know you're armed (and in these modern times, make them feel intimidated and threatened, and make you a lightning rod for attention).

Requiring open carry in the late twentieth century is really a severe limitation on the ability to bear arms.

Other states demand that a legally carried firearm must be completely concealed from sight. Let it show for even a flash (considered terrible etiquette by professionals who regularly carry) and you've violated the law. The definition of *concealed* varies and may include a good deal of discretion.

Handguns typically have stricter carrying requirements than long guns. In Texas, for example, though handgun carry is restricted, long guns are basically unregulated, and it may seem to the casual observer that there is a rifle rack in every pickup truck in the state.

As you can see, equal treatment under the law, demanded by the Constitution in Article IV, the Bill of Rights, and the Fourteenth Amendment, does not seem to apply to state laws.

Prohibited Places

A statewide list of places that can prohibit—or think they can prohibit—an honest citizen with a firearm is one of the hardest things to assemble. No matter how hard you look, there's always the chance of missing one. Every state agency may have enacted its own rules, with or without the proper authority to do so. Rumors abound regarding locations that aren't actually prohibited but that some people believe are off limits. All too often the police will say you can't carry in a place where there is no restriction. Some may even arrest you for a violation that doesn't exist. You get off later and maybe get your gun back. Unfortunately, it happens too frequently.

The authorities should be well aware of their own set of gun rules, but often are not, and should be held accountable when they are in error. Make it your business to know the rules better than they do, so if you are ever in such a situation, you know what your rights are.

Prohibited Possessors

Never forget that it is one hundred percent totally and completely illegal for a criminal to even touch a gun. The federal prohibited possessor list appears in Supplement 2.

Prohibited Weapons

If you're getting a gun for personal safety, you don't have to worry about prohibited weapons. This category typically applies to specially regulated weapons, such as machine guns, sawed-off shotguns, and explosives, things you don't normally think of for personal protection. Any federally licensed gun store can sell you a handgun, rifle, or shotgun—there are thousands to choose from—and you'll be in compliance.

However, laws change and your ability to buy or own a firearm in the future may depend on whether the government, both federal and state, will add to the already huge list of gun laws.

Crime Prevention

States have developed laws and court precedents designed to protect you when you must use force to resist a criminal attack. Some courts have a tendency to frown upon citizens who stand up against criminals. They may take a very narrow reading of the law when determining if you bear guilt in a defensive encounter. "Don't act like a vigilante" is very good advice. However, don't stand around and be victimized either.

Using deadly force in crime prevention is limited to the most violent felony offenses, usually said to include murder, armed robbery, rape, aggravated assault, kidnapping, and arson of an occupied building. In some jurisdictions the list might also include aggravated burglary, certain sexual offenses, and certain property crimes. The justification for using deadly force, or resisting an assault in any manner, is usually more defensible when it happens in your own home, or when innocent life or limb depends on it.

It is not uncommon, when people first stumble upon the crime prevention laws, to think that they've found the key that locks the door on crime. A firearm in your home or carried on your person does not make anyone a freelance police officer. Vigilantism is illegal everywhere, and rightly so. The crime prevention laws are in place so that, if you ever find yourself in an extreme emergency and take drastic action to protect yourself or others, you don't become a criminal by doing so. Hope and pray you never have to rely on a crime prevention law for your defense in your life. And be thankful it's there too.

Trespass

In America, you are generally allowed to insist that a visitor or stranger leave your private property if you wish. You can't discriminate in a place open to the public, and you can't resist the proper authorities if they have legal cause, but for the most part, your rights as a property owner are quite strong.

A person who refuses to leave when asked can be arrested

for trespassing. Some state statutes justify the threat (but not the use) of deadly force to stop a criminal trespass. However, unless the person actually acted to put you in mortal jeopardy you could never legally shoot in such a circumstance.

A situation where you must present a firearm to get someone to leave is a pretty desperate condition, one you should seek to avoid before things go that far. You must also watch out for such laws, because the trespasser, now infuriated, can leave and file charges to make you look like an armed bad guy who made deadly threats for no good reason. You might consider calling the police yourself as soon as your door is locked, to be the first to report the incident.

Felonies and Misdemeanors

A "serious crime" is a *felony* in the eyes of the law. A serious criminal is a *felon*, a serious attack is a *felonious* attack. The worst of the felonies are the crimes that are subject to a deadly force response. Felonies generally require jail terms of more than a year and stiff fines. Convicted felons lose all civil rights: They can't vote or hold public office, sit on a jury, or join the armed forces; they are prohibited from gun ownership or possession, and more. Those are pretty heavy weights to bear.

A misdemeanor is a less serious crime, but it's still pretty serious. It typically carries a maximum sentence of under one year and fines. Some misdemeanors will prevent you from obtaining a firearm permit in some jurisdictions. However, since the passage of the Omnibus Consolidated Appropriations Act of 1997, domestic violence misdemeanor convictions now may prevent you from owning a firearm.

How to Find Your State's Laws

Every state has an official published edition of its laws, in beautifully bound copies, available for sale from an authorized publisher. These sets are very impressive looking, typi-' cally quite expensive, and include annual update services. You can buy single volumes or all of the state statutes, and many publishers are offering editions in computer format, either on-line or on CD-ROMs. Your secretary of state's office can point you to the official publisher.

Agencies within your state may publish and distribute at least some of your state laws, frequently including the main gun laws, for a small fee or even for free (if you can call anything paid for by taxes "free"). Typical offices for getting such copies are the secretary of state, attorney general, district attorney, chief of state police, sheriff, and the main state legislature support office in the capital.

The larger public libraries, special law libraries, law schools, large corporate offices, most branches of government, and even small law offices keep complete sets of state law on hand, with updates (called pocket parts) and notes. The notes include *annotations*, a funny way of saying brief summaries of important cases. Those cases have set precedents that courts are likely to follow. They make fascinating reading, like the heart of a good novel, one after another.

The offices of your elected state representatives can guide you to copies of your state law and may have copies or parts available, sometimes free of charge.

Internet surfers have noticed the rapidly increasing availability of state laws, right down to laws pending before the legislature, on the World Wide Web. The number of states that make their laws available on-line is growing and will, before too long, probably include every state in the Union. State-provided versions are usually without fees; professional on-line providers are quite pricey.

To get an easy-to-read free pamphlet that summarizes your state's gun laws, or to get a list of certified firearm instructors or training counselors, simply write to the oldest and largest firearms training organization in the world, The National Rifle Association, Institute for Legislative Action, 11250 Waples Mill Rd., Fairfax VA 22030, or call (800) 672-3888.

And finally, the Bureau of Alcohol, Tobacco and Firearms publishes a compendium of the basic weapon laws for all fifty states. It is used by dealers nationally to determine the eligibility of customers who wish to purchase firearms. Be careful though, because this book gives the appearance of being complete but is not—it focuses mainly on the laws you must obey, and not the laws that protect your rights or limit the government. Information regarding self-defense is conspicuously absent, as are many rules for carrying or shooting firearms, and other crucial information. However, since it does touch on all fifty states' laws, it is a very handy starting point. To get a free copy of *Firearms: State Laws and Published Ordinances* write ATF Distribution Center, P.O. Box 5950, Springfield, VA 22150, (703) 455-7801, or contact BATF, 650 Massachusetts Ave. NW, Washington, D.C. 20226, (800) 366-5423.

What to Look For

In most states, a full annotated copy of the law is too heavy to lift. In California it fills twenty-seven feet of shelf space. Even if you can get a small-type, no-notes version in just four phone-book-sized volumes, that's a lot of looking just to find the gun laws. They are, by the way, never ever called "gun laws." Key words to search for include: *weapon, firearm, justification, homicide, penal, crime* or *criminal, defense, domestic violence, explosive,* and more.

The main gun laws are usually found in the chapters called "criminal" or "penal" something-or-other. Other gun laws may be found tucked away anywhere in the statutes (frequently called "the codes"—in case there is any doubt about how they are written). For example, in the Commonwealth of Virginia, among the seventeen different titles for gun statutes are "Courts Not of Record" and "Property and Conveyances."

The Baffling "§" Character

What about this funny "§" thing? You see it sprinkled liberally throughout law books. What exactly is that? It's the neatest ingredient for making the law seem alien and unknowable to the average reader. It's the humble section symbol. Every part of the law in every part of the country is called a section. Whenever you see "§," think or say "section." Here's the trick for writing a section symbol: Make a capital "S" on top of, and halfway down, another capital "S."

Now that you know what the symbol means, you can make sense of every formerly mysterious cross-reference in the law. Look for capital letters nearby, which are an abbreviation for the title of the book that contains the piece (make that section) of law. It can actually get to be quite fun, deciphering the bafflegab our legislators use to obscure our laws. Sometimes, to keep things hopping, sections are called articles, or parts. And if things start getting too plain, maybe they throw in some Latin for good measure. Easy. Don't let it confound you ever again.

A Word About Preemption

Forty-two states have laws that, in theory at least, allow only the state legislature to pass further gun control legislation. Such laws are enacted to help maintain a statewide uniformity of firearms laws. In many places, however, local ordinances have been grandfathered into effect, and localities may retain some gun-law legislative powers. Instead of getting equal treatment under the law, many citizens face a bewildering glut of petty regulations, like a Gordian knot, even within their own state.

States that have wisely adopted effective preemption do their residents a service. Your state would do well to adopt comprehensive preemption if it doesn't already have it. Then we can look further to the problem of disjointed laws in neighboring states for those of us who dare venture out of state in, say, a car.

The Lost National Right to Carry

There once was a time when you could carry a gun with you when you traveled. Today your right to travel with a firearm is all but lost if you leave your home state. It takes inordinate effort to find out what all the laws are, and you can be arrested for a technical violation that wouldn't be illegal back home. Quite a few honest citizens are traveling around today, not knowing if they can legally own or carry their firearms.

And you can just hear the real criminals laughing in the background. Wouldn't it make sense for the citizens of each state to be entitled to all the privileges and immunities of citizens in the several states? That's precisely what the Constitution calls for in Article IV.

The federal government, with all its resources, cannot be fully cognizant of all the nuances of the laws in all fifty states and thousands of localities, so how on earth could you?

Law-abiding Americans want to comply, they are eager to comply, they don't want to be in violation. They go out of their way to find out what the laws actually are. They buy books like this one. These are not the gun owners that non-gun owners should worry about. These are the good guys—they are you and I.

People who decide to be able to defend themselves face a risk. It is the risk of succumbing to an attack or succumbing to the legal system. This little odyssey through the labyrinth of the laws should make each of us pause, but should not stop anyone from exercising their rights—especially *the inalienable right to self-defense*. Because for all its shortcomings, and all the severe risks involved in a deadly confrontation, the law is basically good and on your side. Legitimate self-defense is universally recognized, and after all, self-defense is the primary civil right.

The following chart is attached for reference.

COMPENDIUM OF STATE LAWS GOVERNING FIREARMS

The following chart lists the main provisions of state firearms laws as of the date of publication. In addition to the state provisions, the purchase, sale, and, in certain circumstances, the possession and interstate transportation of firearms are regulated by the Federal Gun Control Act of 1968 as amended by the Firearms Owners' Protection Act of 1986. Also, cities and localities may have their own gun ordinances in addition to federal and state restrictions. Details may be obtained by contacting local law enforcement authorities or by consulting your state's firearms law digest compiled by the NRA Institute for Legislative Action.

STATE	GUN BAN	INSTANT CHECK	FEDERAL WAITING PERIOD APPLIES[11]	STATE WAITING PERIOD - NUMBER OF DAYS		LICENSE OR PERMIT TO PURCHASE		REGISTRATION		RECORD OF SALE REPORTED TO STATE OR LOCAL GOVT.
				HANDGUNS	LONG GUNS	HANDGUNS	LONG GUNS	HANDGUNS	LONG GUNS	
Alabama	—	—	X	2	—	—	—	—	—	X
Alaska	—	—	X[23]	—	—	—	—	—	—	—
Arizona	—	X[3]	X[23]	—	—	—	—	—	—	—
Arkansas	—	—	X	—	—	—	—	—	—	X
California	X[22]	—	—	15	15	—	—	—	—	—
Colorado	—	X[3]	—	—	—	—	—	—	—	X
Connecticut	X[22]	—	—	14[16,17]	14[16,17]	—	—	—	—	—
Delaware	—	X[3]	—	—	—	—	—	—	—	—
Florida	—	X[3]	—	3[16,17]	—	—	—	—	—	—
Georgia	X[22]	X[3]	—	—	—	—	—	—	—	—
Hawaii	—	—	—	—	—	X[18]	X[18]	X[14]	X[14]	X
Idaho	—	X[3,23]	23	—	—	—	—	—	—	—
Illinois	22	X	—	3	1	X[18]	X[18]	—[4]	—[4]	X
Indiana	—	—	—	7[17]	—	X[18]	—	—	—	X
Iowa	—	—	—	—	—	—	—	—	—	X
Kansas	—	—	X	1	—	1	—	—[1]	—	—
Kentucky	—	—	X[23]	—	—	—	—	—	—	—
Louisiana	—	—	X[23]	—	—	—	—	—	—	—

State	1	2	3	4	5	6	7	8	9	10
Maine								X		
Maryland	X			X_{18}	X_{18}	7_9	7			X_{22}
Massachusetts	X			X_{18}	X_{18}		7			
Michigan	X		X		X_{18}	18	7_{18}			
Minnesota	X						7			
Mississippi					X_{18}			X_{23}		
Missouri	X							X_{23}		
Montana								X		
Nebraska			-						$1C$	
Nevada				X_{18}	X_{10}				X_{12}	
New Hampshire	X			18				X	X	
New Jersey	X	X	X		X_{18}					X_{22}
New Mexico		7						X		
New York	X		-							22
North Carolina	X				X_{18}			X_{23}		
North Dakota	X				X_{18}			X		22
Ohio	-				18		1	X		
Oklahoma										
Oregon	X								X	
Pennsylvania	X					7	$2,0$	10	$1D$	
Rhode Island	X						7	X	X	
South Carolina	X				8		8	X		
South Dakota	X						2	X_{23}		
Tennessee	X						15			
Texas								X	X	
Utah									X	
Vermont								X		
Virginia	-				$1,E$		$1,8$	X	X	X_{22}
Washington	X						$5,12$	X	X	
West Virginia								X		
Wisconsin	X						2	X	X	
Wyoming								X		
District of Columbia	X	X	X_{18}	X_{18}	X_{18}					X_{22}

Since state laws are subject to frequent change, this chart is not to be considered legal advice or a restatement of the law.

All fifty states have now passed sportsmen's protections laws to halt harrassment.

STATE	STATE PROVISION FOR RIGHT-TO-CARRY CONCEALED[15]	CARRYING OPENLY PROHIBITED	OWNER ID CARDS OR LICENSING	FIREARM RIGHTS CONSTITUTIONAL PROVISION	STATE FIREARMS PREEMPTION LAWS	RANGE PROTECTION LAW
Alabama	R	X[13]	—	X	X[25]	—
Alaska	R	—	—	X	—	—
Arizona	R	—	—	X	X	—
Arkansas	R	X[5]	—	X	X	—
California	L	X[6]	—	—	X	—
Colorado	L	—	—	X	—	—
Connecticut	R	X	—	X	X[19]	—
Delaware	L	—	—	X	X	—
Florida	R	X	—	X	X	—
Georgia	R	X	—	X	X	—
Hawaii	L	X	X	X	—	—
Idaho	R	—	—	X	X	X
Illinois	D	X	X	—	—	X
Indiana	R	X	—	X	X[20]	X
Iowa	L	X	—	—	X	—
Kansas	D	—[1]	—	X	—	—
Kentucky	R	—	—	X	X	—
Louisiana	R	—	—	X	X	—
Maine	R	—	—	X	X	X

State						
Maryland	L	X			X	
Massachusetts	L	X	X	X	X[19]	X
Michigan	L	X[13]		X	X	X
Minnesota	L	X			X	
Mississippi	R			X	X	
Missouri	D			X	X	X
Montana	R			X	X	X
Nebraska	D			X		
Nevada	R			X	X	
New Hampshire	R	X	X			X
New Jersey	L			X	X[19]	X
New Mexico	D	X	X		X	
New York	L			X	X[19]	X
North Carolina	R	X[6]		X	X	
North Dakota	R			X	X	
Ohio	D	−[5]	[8]	X		
Oklahoma	R	X[5]		X	X	X
Oregon	R			X	X	X
Pennsylvania	R	X[13]		X	X	X
Rhode Island	L	X		X	X	
South Carolina	R	X		X	X	
South Dakota	R			X	X	
Tennessee	R	X[5]		X	X	X
Texas	R	X		X	X	
Utah	R[21]	X[6]		X	X	
Vermont	R	X[5]		X	X	X
Virginia	R			X	X	X
Washington	R	X[24]		X	X	
West Virginia	R			X	X	
Wisconsin	D				X	
Wyoming	R			X	X	X
District of Columbia	D	X	X	NA		

With over 20,000 "gun control" laws on the books in America, there are two challenges facing every gun owner.

First, you owe it to yourself to become familiar with the federal laws on gun ownership. Only by knowing the laws can you avoid innocently breaking one.

Second, while federal legislation receives much more media attention, state legislatures and city councils make many more decisions regarding your right to own and carry firearms. NRA members and all gun owners must take extra care to be aware of anti-gun laws and ordinances at the state and local levels.

Notes:

1. In certain cities or counties.

2. **Nevada** has, but does not use, its Instant Check system.

3. Concealed firearm carry permit holders are exempt from Instant Check. In **Idaho**, not all licensed firearm dealers participate with the Instant Check system.

4. Chicago only. No handgun not already registered may be lawfully possessed.

5. **Arkansas** prohibits carrying a firearm "with a purpose to employ it as a weapon against a person." **Tennessee** prohibits carrying "with the intent to go armed." **Vermont** prohibits carrying a firearm "with the intent or purpose of injuring another."

6. Loaded.

7. New York City only.

8. A permit is required to acquire another handgun before 30 days have elapsed following the acquisition of a handgun.

9. **Maryland** subjects purchases of "assault weapons" to a 7-day waiting period.

10. Instant check is not yet operational. **Nebraska:** When Instant Check is operational, firearm purchases from licensed dealers will be subject either

owners must possess a Firearms Owner's ID Card (FID) or a license to carry. Handgun purchasers must have a (a) license to carry, or (b) purchase permit and an FID, or (c) purchase permit and proof of exempt status. A handgun permit is valid for 10 days. A long gun purchaser must have a carry license or FID or proof of exempt status. **Michigan:** A handgun purchaser must obtain a license to purchase from local law enforcement, and within 10 days present the license and handgun to obtain a certificate of inspection. **Minnesota:** A handgun transfer or carrying permit, or a 7-day waiting period and handgun transfer report, is required to purchase handguns or "assault weapons" from a dealer. A permit or transfer report must be issued to qualified applicants within 7 days. A permit is valid for one year, a transfer report for 30 days. **Missouri:** A purchase permit is required for a handgun, must be issued to qualified applicants within 7 days, and is valid for 30 days. **New Jersey:** Firearm owners must possess an FID, which must be issued to qualified applicants within 30 days. To purchase a handgun, an FID and a purchase permit, which must be issued within 30 days to qualified applicants, is valid for 90 days, are required. An FID is required to purchase long guns. **New York:** Purchase, possession and/or carrying of a handgun require a single license, which includes any restrictions made upon the bearer. New York City also requires a license for long guns. **North Carolina:** To purchase a handgun, a license or permit is required, which must be issued to qualified applicants within 30 days. **Ohio:** Some cities require a permit-to-purchase or firearm owner ID card.

19. Preemption through judicial ruling. Local regulation may be instituted in **Massachusetts** if ratified by the legislature.

20. Except Gary and East Chicago and local laws enacted before January, 1994.

to it or the current permit-to-purchase, at the purchaser's option. **Pennsylvania**: When Instant Check is operational, the state waiting period will end and the Federal waiting period will no longer apply. Carry permit holders will be exempt from Instant Check.

11. As interpreted by the Bureau of Alcohol, Tobacco and Firearms.

12. May be extended by police to 30 days in some circumstances. An individual not holding a driver's license must wait 90 days.

13. Carrying a handgun openly in a motor vehicle requires a license.

14. Every person arriving in **Hawaii** is required to register any firearm(s) brought into the State within 3 days of arrival of the person or firearm(s) whichever occurs later. Handguns purchased from licensed dealers must be registered within 5 days.

15. Concealed carry laws vary significantly between the states. Ratings reflect the real effect a state's particular laws have on the ability of citizens to carry firearms for self-defense.

16. Purchases from licensed dealers only

17. The state waiting period does not apply to a person holding a valid permit or license to carry a firearm. In **Connecticut**, a hunting license also exempts the holder, for long gun purchases. In **Indiana**, only persons with unlimited carry permits are exempt.

18. **District of Columbia**: No handgun may be possessed unless it was registered prior to Sept. 23, 1976 and re-registered by Feb 5, 1977. A permit to purchase is required for a rifle or shotgun. **Hawaii**: Purchase permits, required for all firearms, may not be issued until 14 days after application. A handgun purchase permit is valid for 10 days, for one handgun; a long gun permit is valid for one year, for multiple long guns. **Illinois**: A Firearm Owner's Identification Card (FOID) is required to possess or purchase a firearm, must be issued to qualified applicants within 30 days, and is valid for 5 years. **Iowa**: A purchase permit is required for handguns, and is valid for one year, beginning three days after issuance. **Massachusetts**: Firearm

21. **Vermont** law respects your right to carry without a permit.

22. **California, Connecticut, New Jersey, New York City**, other local jurisdictions in New York, and some local jurisdictions in Ohio prohibit "assault weapons." **Hawaii** prohibits "assault pistols. **Illinois**: Chicago, Evanston, Oak Park, Morton Grove, Winnetka, Wilmette, and Highland Park prohibit handguns; some cities prohibit other kinds of firearms. **Maryland** prohibits several small, low-caliber, inexpensive handguns and "assault pistols." **Ohio**: some cities prohibit handguns of certain magazine capacities." **Virginia** prohibits "Street Sweeper" shotguns. The **District of Columbia** prohibits new acquisition of handguns and any semi-automatic firearm capable of using a detachable ammunition magazine of more than 12 rounds capacity. (With respect to some of these laws and ordinances, individuals may retain prohibited firearms owned previously, with certain restrictions.)

23. The Federal waiting period does not apply to a person holding a valid permit or license to carry a firearm, issued within 5 years of proposed purchase. In Idaho the Federal waiting period applies to purchases of handguns from licensed dealers not participating with the state's Instant Check system.

24. Local jurisdictions may opt out of prohibition.

25. Preemption only applies to handguns.

Concealed carry codes:

R: Right-to-Carry: "shall issue" or less restrictive discretionary permit system (Ala., Conn.) (See also note #21.)

L: Right-to-Carry Limited by local authority's discretion over permit issuance.

D: Right-to-Carry Denied, no permit system exists; concealed carry is prohibited.

Rev.1/97 15m

REFERENCES

Texts

Ayoob, Massad. *In the Gravest Extreme*. Police Bookshelf, 1980.

Cottrol, Robert J., ed., *Gun Control and the Constitution: Sources and Explorations on the Second Amendment*. Garland Publishing, 1994.

Halbrook, Stephen P., *That Every Man Be Armed*. Independent Institute, 1994.

Kopel, David B. *The Samurai, the Mountie and the Cowboy*. Prometheus Books, 1992.

LaPierre, Wayne. *Guns, Crime and Freedom*. Regnery Publishing, 1994.

Quigley, Paxton. *Armed and Female*. St. Martin's Press, 1993.

Walker, Lenore E. *Terrifying Love: Why Battered Women Kill and How Society Responds*. HarperCollins, 1990.

Case Law and Statutes

American Jurisprudence, Bancroft Whitney
Arizona Revised Statutes

Code of Federal Regulations

Code of Virginia

Corpus Juris Segundum, West Publishing

Department of the Treasury, Bureau of Alcohol, Tobacco and Firearms, *Federal Firearms Regulations Reference Guide*. Washington, D.C.: GPO, 1995.

Supreme Court Digest, West Publishing

United States Code

United States Supreme Court Reporter (Case Decisions): *Acers v. United States*, 1896; *Alberty v. United States*, 1896; *Allen v. United States*, 1896; *Allison v. United States*, 1895; *Beard v. United States*, 1895; *Brown v. United States*, 1921; *Gourko v. United States*, 1894; *Rowe v. United States*, 1896; *Thompson v. United States*, 1894; *Wallace v. United States*, 1896.

Vernon's Texas Civil Statutes, West Publishing

Other Sources

Encyclopedia Americana

Encyclopedia Brittanica

Federal Bureau of Investigation, Uniform Crime Reports

United States Department of Justice, Bureau of Justice Statistics

Selected materials were graciously provided by Bloomfield Press from their titles: *The Arizona Gun Owner's Guide*, *The Texas Gun Owner's Guide*, *The Virginia Gun Owner's Guide*, and *Gun Laws of America: Every Federal Gun Law on the Books*.

INDEX